The Manager's Pocket Guide to Mega Thinking and Planning

Roger Kaufman, Ph.D., CPT

HRD Press, Inc. • Amherst • Massachusetts

Copyright © 2011 by Roger Kaufman

HRD Press, Inc.
22 Amherst Road
Amherst, Massachusetts 01002
1-800-822-2801 (U.S. and Canada)
(413) 253-3488
(413) 253-3490 (fax)
http://www.hrdpress.com

No part of the material should be reproduced or utilized in any form or by any means, electronic or mechanical, including photocopying, recording, or by information storage and retrieval systems, without written permission from the publisher.

ISBN 978-1-59996-251-1

Production services by Jean Miller
Cover design by Eileen Klockars
Editorial services by Sally Farnham

The Manager's Pocket Guide to Mega Thinking and Planning

Acknowledgements iii

What this Book Will Do for You 1

Chapter 1: The Basic Concepts Required to Define Success Using Mega Thinking and Planning 9

Chapter 2: The Organizational Elements Model: Ensuring that We Work at the Correct Level 21

Chapter 3: The Ideal Vision: Selecting Where You Are Headed and Justifying Why You Want to Get There 33

Chapter 4: Six Critical Success Factors for Successful Mega Thinking and Planning 55

Chapter 5: Objectives and Performance Specifications: The Criteria for Accomplishment 63

Chapter 6: Mission Objectives: Preparing the Objective for Your Organization 81

Chapter 7: Needs and Needs Assessment 87

Chapter 8: Implementing the Mega Plan 127

Chapter 9: Evaluation and Continual Improvement: What Worked, What Didn't, What to Keep, and What to Change 155

Chapter 10: Some Final Guidance 173

Glossary of Terms 193

About the Author 203

Acknowledgments

I appreciate the critical reviews of earlier drafts provided by Dr. Ingrid-Guerra Lopez and Dr. Mariano Bernardez. They made this work better than it would have been otherwise, but flaws still remain mine. I also acknowledge the increasing number of professionals who are applying Mega Thinking and Planning and provide the practical implementation data that is required for continual improvement.

I am indebted to Robert Carkhuff and HRD Press for having confidence in the practical importance of Mega Thinking and Planning to not only publish this work but a six-pack series on Mega, the Assessment Book, that guides people to decide to use the approach, as well as an "applied Mega" series. Sally Farnham has done an outstanding job of editing although any problems or errors are strictly mine. The entire staff of HRD Press also earns my praise for helping the guide be better than it would have been if left entirely up to me.

What This Book Will Do for You

Planning is just a substitute for good luck. If you can count on having good luck then you don't have to bother with rigorous results-oriented planning. Most of us don't depend on luck, especially in a dynamic world.

Because the future is uncertain, Peter Drucker's advice that "if you can't predict the future, create it" is useful. Creating that better future is the subject of this book. You can be successful and the choice to do so is up to you.

This book

- allows you to identify opportunities and problems in order for you to define and deliver personal and organizational success;
- provides the key concepts for you to justify what to change and what to continue in your organization;
- provides practical and proven tools for successful strategic thinking and planning; and
- gives you what is required to define and deliver success and to be able to prove the value that you are adding to the organization, clients, and our shared world.

If you don't want to succeed, there are many popular approaches available to you, but before you choose to follow the leader, do look at the wreckage of contemporary organizations—from Wall Street to Main Street and from Washington, D.C., to your home town—that will stand witness to the fact that "popular strategic planning" approaches are not necessarily "effective."

The approach provided in this book works and has been successfully applied around most of the world. This proven approach looks at wholes and not parts; it looks at the entire system, not "systems" in isolation from all other organizational parts as well as the overarching purpose of the organization. When we look at the organization in the context of external clients and our shared society, that is a "system approach" and not a "systems approach" that fragments the various pieces and parts and usually treats them as if they were the only variable that is important.

For example, when we seek a surgeon, we are not only interested in his or her skills and training, but also must be concerned with his or her success in returning patients to a healthy life; we go beyond how the surgeon practices to also be concerned about his or her success. Another example of the important distinction involving looking at the whole and not just the parts is demonstrated in Chapter 9. Instead of only looking at individual "systems" of a city, such as housing or water and sewage, all such subsystems are assessed both individually as well as in interaction with all others to deliver a common good: the health, safety, and welfare of all residents. For example, one could fix the water supply and distribution of a city and leave the rest of the city in jeopardy by not all looking at other important variables such as crime, poverty, transportation, jobs, or electrical services. What we suggest, a holistic or system approach, is a shift away from the conventional single-issue politics and planning.

When we do planning, there are some realities for us to consider. One is that the world is not divided into individual jobs, organizational sections, divisions, policies, laws, rules, or regulations. It is not divided into splinters or "systems." We should examine the total organization as well as its social context, for organizations are just means to societal ends.

Another reality is that we cannot solve today's problems with the same thinking and tools that caused the current problems; we must be open to new ways of thinking and managing. Also, we should not stop at being the best of the best; we must be the only one who does what we do and deliver. Because of these new realities, we provide an alternative to conventional wisdom and methods.

Our world is changing and is changeable. Successful planning will define where we should head, justify why we should go there, and provide the criteria for judging our progress and success.

Our challenge is to create the future of our organization and its partners. Before talking about the practical tools and techniques for successful planning, we first define the full landscape

What This Book Will Do for You

of planning and delivery of success in which these tools must contribute.

Some basics about this approach to keep in mind include the following:

- Mega Thinking and Planning[1] has a primary focus on our shared society to which we must contribute. While other approaches don't deal with the society where all of us live, this strategy will and it will deliver unique success.

- There is a fundamental difference between ends (or results, consequences, or impacts) and means (processes, activities, programs, projects, funding, and resources). This emphasis on ends, results, and consequences is throughout successful Mega Thinking and Planning.

- Needs are not the same as wants. Needs are gaps in results—gaps between current results and desired results. This is a part of another basic concept; a focus on ends and not means.

- There are three levels of organizational results: societal, organizational, and individual. They must all be included and linked.

Navigating the Minefields of Conventional Wisdom and Sloppy Thinking

Now is the right time to clear up some commonly used concepts and words that are still popular but won't work well for you. Let's look at some common but potentially damaging things that can get in the way of your success.

Words and what they actually mean are central to successful planning, so let me ask for your thoughtfulness since the words we use will have the precision and rigor required to define and deliver success. After all, planning and organizational success and the rigor associated with it is different from that of Humpty Dumpty who told Alice that "when I use a word it means just what I choose it to mean—neither more nor less."[2] There is a glossary of terms at the end of this book, so you never have to feel lost.

Here are the basics of this approach:

a) There are three levels of planning and three levels of results. From conventional usage, every result is an "outcome" and every level of planning is "strategic," and that is not true.[3] Table 2.1 in Chapter 2 provides a useful relation.

b) You can do useful strategic thinking and planning for every area of your organization, including manufacturing, human resources, shipping, and marketing. Planning fails when you fail to knit all parts of your organization together to add value to external clients and our shared society.[4]

c) "Needs" are portrayed as something you really have to have; that is not a "need," it is a "want." Most needs assessments are wants assessments and will be wrong about 80+ percent of the time.

d) Mega is *not* shorthand for "really big," Macro is *not* code for "big," and Micro is *not* code for "small." Mega is societal, Macro is organizational, and Micro is individual or small group. It is not about size, but focus. Using comfortable words might be tempting, but doing so will likely keep you from really defining and delivering success.

Mega Thinking and Planning can deliver success to you, your organization, your external clients, and our shared world if you will use it and apply it properly. You are in charge of your own success and future. What is offered here about strategic thinking and planning using Mega Planning will provide you with useful options for you to select. But it is different from the conventional approaches. (If it was not, why should you bother?)

This *Manager's Pocket Guide to Mega Thinking and Planning*[5] is based on what has been successfully applied around the world, yet is different from "standard" approaches taught in most business schools and those we read about every day—the ones that have led to the Gulf of Mexico pollution disaster, Enron, 9/11, financial meltdowns, bursting of the tech bubble and then the housing bubble, among many others. Because of the failure of

What This Book Will Do for You

conventional approaches, Mega Thinking and Planning provides the opportunity for you to be correct in an atmosphere of the failure of other approaches. So instead of following the leader, this will allow you to be the leader by adding value to yourself, your organization, and our shared society.

The simple truth is that conventional approaches to strategic thinking and planning—the ones taught and those quoted in newspapers, magazines, and journals are flawed.[6] Using them will make you appear to be "in the mainstream" but will likely lead to drowning. Here is what they miss and we do not:

- All organizations are means to societal ends, and thus successful strategic thinking—*Mega* Thinking and Planning—starts with a primary focus on adding value for all stakeholders, including our shared society. It is pragmatic, realistic, practical, and ethical. The conventional approaches, ones you should avoid, start with the organization (and its profit-and-loss sheet for the coming quarterly report) as the primary client and beneficiary and miss considering the impact on where you and I live and work: society.

- Organizations tend to be structured in individual silos—departments, bureaus, groups—and these splintered organizations cannot look to the common good but tend to optimize on their own funding and political survival. Budgets are allocated to functions and not to common results. From this comes internal competition for resources instead of cooperation based on a common destination upon which resources will be allocated. This is also true for federal, state, and local governments.

- Conventional tools for planning, design, implementation, and evaluation are based on an incomplete view of what organizations must deliver, so using them will maintain the status quo but not deliver success for you and your organization.

The Manager's Pocket Guide to Mega Thinking and Planning

The intention of this book is to provide you with a viable approach to planning—Mega Thinking and Planning—so that you won't repeat the failed or failing ways that are tempting everyone in the field. All that is asked is for you to carefully consider the definitions and meanings of words and concepts here and not automatically think this is semantic quibbling or just another way of saying things. Just as you want your physician to be very precise about what he uses and does, so do all of those you deal with expect precision, rigor, and competence from you.

Defining and achieving continual personal and organizational success is possible. It relies on three basic elements:

- a societal value-added "frame of mind" (your way of thinking, your perspective and commitment about your organization, people, and our shared world)
- shared determination and agreement on where to head and why (everyone who can or might be affected by the shared objectives must agree on purposes and results criteria)
- pragmatic and basic tools

Action Steps

1. Decide to be successful and create your future and not accept at face value the existing popular approaches and models for "strategic planning."

2. Personally adopt a frame of mind that you will add measurable value to yourself, your organization, and our shared society.

3. Continue questioning things, keep an open mind, and continue with the rest of this book.

What This Book Will Do for You

Endnotes

1. Mega Thinking and Planning has been evolving for many years, perhaps first formally with Kaufman's 1972 *Educational System Planning* (Prentice Hall) and further developed in Kaufman & English, 1979 (Educational Technology), and continuing through today. In one form or another, using a societal frame for planning and doing has shown up in the works of respected thinkers, including Senge and more recently Prahalad and Davis. Recent work by Mariano Bernardez has provide additional substance for measuring Mega Planning results and consequences.

2. Lewis Carroll, 1872. *Through the Looking Glass.*

3. Now, when someone mumbles "learning outcomes," you will make a note that they are really talking about "learning products" and they likely have failed to link the learning results with organizational results (Macro/ Outputs) and those to external client and societal contributions (Mega/ Outcomes).

4. A number of years ago I was asked to review all of the "strategic" plans created by each of the commonwealth agencies in Australia. Using Mega as the baseline, I reported back publicly that the plans varied from inadequate to awful. Then I added "but that is not what really worries me. What really bothers me is if each agency is doing their own strategic plan, who is doing the strategic plan for Australia?" That landed me on the Australian magazine cover of *Directions in Government* with the headline "Where is the Mega Plan?" *Directions in Government.* (June, 1989). Where's the Mega Plan? Interview with Roger Kaufman, Sydney, Australia.

5. This guide builds on much of my previous work, including:

    Kaufman, R. (2006). *30 Seconds that can change your life: A decision-making guide for those who refuse to be mediocre.* Amherst, MA: HRD Press, Inc.

Kaufman, R. (2006). *Change, choices, and consequences: A guide to Mega Thinking and Planning.* Amherst, MA: HRD Press, Inc.

Kaufman, R., & Guerra-Lopez, I. (2008). *The assessment book: Applied strategic thinking and performance improvement through self-assessments.* Amherst, MA: HRD Press, Inc.

6. Stewart, M. (2009). *The management myth: Why the "experts" keep getting it wrong.* New York: W. W. Norton.

   Kaufman, R. (March–April, 2010). Review of *The management myth: Why the "experts" keep getting it wrong.* (W. W. Norton, 2009). *Educational Technology,* pp. 48–50.

Chapter 1

The Basic Concepts Required to Define Success Using Mega Thinking and Planning

Your success and your organization's success are possible, practical and ethical.[1] It depends on you and your commitment to defining useful results and orchestrating the resources, methods, and products to get from where you are to where you want to be. Continuing success depends on adding value to our shared world.

Success—getting the rewards for your job being well done—is simply a matter of aligning what you use, do, produce, and deliver to adding value both inside and outside of your organization.

Mega Thinking and Planning Defined

Adding value to our shared society using your organization as the primary vehicle is the purpose and defining characteristic of Mega Thinking and Planning.[2] When we place our shared world—where we live with others—as primary, that is Mega Planning. From this shared societal value-added framework, everything you use, do, produce, and deliver will achieve agreed-on positive organizational as well as societal results.

If you are not adding value to our shared society, you have no assurance that you are not subtracting value. Every organization should ask and answer the following central question that puts into perspective you, your organization, and the overall purpose you work toward:

> **If my organization is the solution, what's the problem?**

This Mega focus for strategic thinking and planning represents a shift from the usual attention on oneself, individual performance improvement, and one's organization to making certain you also add value to external clients and society.

Preview of Three Guides for Defining and Delivering Success

Of course, you will work with others to define and deliver success. In order for you to play your part, there are three guides that, when they become second nature to you, will allow you to define and achieve success:

Guide 1: The Organizational Elements Model (OEM). The elements Mega, Macro, Micro, Process, and Input (see Table 2.1) identify the basic questions every organization should ask and answer. It is important to define and link (align) what any organization uses, does, produces, and delivers to achieve external client and societal value added. The OEM, then, helps you do this.

This first guide helps you make sure that everything you use, do, produce, and deliver adds measurable value within and outside of your organization. It is also a diagnostic tool—it will provide you the data on the "vital signs" of your organization that may be used to sort any idea, intervention, or approach into it and find out what it is in the context of what the organization uses, does, produces, delivers, as well as the external value it adds.

Any time you are deciding to consider, use, or do something, sort it into the OEM and thus make sure it will integrate and align with all the Organizational Elements.

Guide 2: The Ideal Vision: Agreeing on where to head and why you want to get there. The Ideal Vision—a measurable statement agreed to by all partners—defines the kind of world we want to help create for tomorrow's child (Figure 2.1). This measurable "North Star" will allow you and others to correctly navigate individually and together toward a useful destination. The Ideal Vision allows you to ensure that everything you use, do, produce, and deliver adds measurable value to all stakeholders, including our shared society. As the name implies, it is an "ideal," and we might not get there soon, or even in our lifetime, but it is practical in that it provides a commitment and focus on continually moving toward the world we want to create for tomorrow's child. If that is not where we want to head, then where should we go?

Define Success Using Mega Thinking and Planning

The focus on societal consequences is what is missing from other strategic thinking and planning approaches. Because there is no societal value-added focus, public and private organizations frequently go into crisis: they, unfortunately, exclude societal good in favor of short-term financial gains.[3]

The Ideal Vision is essential in making sure those diverse groups, within and outside of your organization, agree on the common destination to which they may uniquely contribute; it allows for the integration and cooperation of all partners.

Guide 3: Six critical success factors that define the realities of successful Mega Thinking and Planning. These are the factors that will guide you and keep you on target as you define where to head, justify why you want to get there, and manage the process successfully (Table 4.1).

Measurable results—results that add value for all stakeholders—are basic to successful planning. Making money and doing organizational and societal good should not be mutually exclusive.

Change, Choice, and Consequences

You are, like everyone else, what you do and deliver, and what you deliver is very public and noticeable.

Success is a choice—the ever-present reality of *Change*, the *Choices* you make, and the *Consequences* of those choices.

- Change
- Choice
- Consequences

You get what you plan and work for....

Change. Change is scary for most of us. We know how to deal with today. Some would rather deal with current reality rather than getting out of their comfort zones and take a risk to change what we do and how we act. As counter-intuitive as it might at first sound, change can be quick if only we find the right incentives for people to change.[4] One only has to identify those rewards that make it practical for people to change. Major changes have happened very rapidly when the consequences of change appear as worthwhile to people.

Choice. We do make choices; not making a choice is a choice. We can be the masters of change or the victims. No matter our choices, the consequences are ours to own. We have to commit to our choices and carry them through until we get the results we desire.

Consequences. What happens to us is largely up to us. If bad things happen, we can be resilient and learn, or give up and drift from day-to-day. *Means*—our choices about how to change—lead to *ends*, results, and consequences. It seems smart to link our choices to the consequences we want and not leave it up to others to decide for us.

The basic choice for any planning is the frame of reference for our primary client and beneficiary we use. There are three options:

- our external clients and society as the primary beneficiary of everything we use, do, produce, and deliver (This is called the *Mega* level.)
- our organization as the primary beneficiary (This is called the *Macro* level.)

or

- our workgroup[5] as the primary beneficiary (This is called the *Micro* level.)

If you choose other than Mega as the primary client and beneficiary—external clients and society—then you are assuming that everything you use, do, and deliver will be worthy to those who judge our success, including our neighbors and our shared world.

Think for a moment: don't we all depend on everyone we deal with—from supermarkets to physicians, to car manufacturers and restaurants, to airlines—to be first focused on our survival and well-being? They should be able to rely on us for the same.

Define Success Using Mega Thinking and Planning

Choosing Mega Thinking and Planning: Important Variables to Consider

Success involves defining what you want to accomplish, justifying what you intend to accomplish, and getting from where you are to the destination. To understand and internalize what you are about to do (or not to do), here is an assessment instrument[6] is provided in Table 1.1. This assessment will let you identify **What Is** and compare that to **What Should Be** to define and commit to Mega Thinking and Planning (as distinguished from conventional approaches).

Filling this out, either by yourself or with your planning partners, will also give you a "preview of coming attractions" in terms of concepts and words that this book provides. If there are terms that are not clear, skip those items (or look them up in the Glossary) for now, knowing you will be clear about them and their value by the end of this book.

WHAT IS					STRATEGIC THINKING AND PLANNING SURVEY	WHAT SHOULD BE				
1 - Rarely, if ever	2 - Not usually	3 - Sometimes	4 - Frequently	5 - Consistently	Respond to each item below using the following scale. Use this scale for both What Is and What Should Be. 1 – Rarely, if ever 2 – Not usually 3 – Sometimes 4 – Frequently 5 – Consistently	1 - Rarely, if ever	2 - Not usually	3 - Sometimes	4 - Frequently	5 - Consistently
①	②	③	④	⑤	1. Planning has a focus on creating the future.	①	②	③	④	⑤
①	②	③	④	⑤	2. We define *strategic planning* as starting with an initial focus on measurable societal value added.	①	②	③	④	⑤
①	②	③	④	⑤	3. We define *tactical planning* as having a focus on measurable organizational value added.	①	②	③	④	⑤
①	②	③	④	⑤	4. We define *operational planning* as having a focus on measurable individual and small group value added.	①	②	③	④	⑤

(continued)

The Manager's Pocket Guide to Mega Thinking and Planning

Respond to each item below using the following scale. Use this scale for both **What Is** and **What Should Be**.

1 – Rarely, if ever
2 – Not usually
3 – Sometimes
4 – Frequently
5 – Consistently

WHAT IS	STRATEGIC THINKING AND PLANNING SURVEY	WHAT SHOULD BE
① ② ③ ④ ⑤	5. We **start** *strategic planning and thinking* at the societal value-added level.	① ② ③ ④ ⑤
① ② ③ ④ ⑤	6. In our strategic planning, we carefully distinguish among strategic, tactical, and operational planning.	① ② ③ ④ ⑤
① ② ③ ④ ⑤	7. We align—link and relate—strategic, tactical, and operational planning.	① ② ③ ④ ⑤
① ② ③ ④ ⑤	8. All people in our organization understand the differences and relationships among strategic, tactical, and operational planning.	① ② ③ ④ ⑤
① ② ③ ④ ⑤	9. Planning involves, either directly or indirectly, all those people and parties who will be impacted by the results of the strategic plan.	① ② ③ ④ ⑤
① ② ③ ④ ⑤	10. Planning always focuses on results.	① ② ③ ④ ⑤
① ② ③ ④ ⑤	11. Planning has always focused on the consequences of achieving (or not achieving) results.	① ② ③ ④ ⑤
① ② ③ ④ ⑤	12. Planning is proactive.	① ② ③ ④ ⑤
① ② ③ ④ ⑤	13. Revisions to the plan are made any time it is required.	① ② ③ ④ ⑤
① ② ③ ④ ⑤	14. We use an Ideal Vision—the kind of world we want to help create for tomorrow's child—as the basis for planning.	① ② ③ ④ ⑤
① ② ③ ④ ⑤	15. People who are involved and could be impacted by the plans participate in the planning.	① ② ③ ④ ⑤

(continued)

Define Success Using Mega Thinking and Planning

Respond to each item below using the following scale. Use this scale for both **What Is** and **What Should Be**.

1 – Rarely, if ever
2 – Not usually
3 – Sometimes
4 – Frequently
5 – Consistently

WHAT IS	STRATEGIC THINKING AND PLANNING SURVEY	WHAT SHOULD BE
① ② ③ ④ ⑤	16. We use a formal needs assessment—collecting and prioritizing gaps in results—for making plans.	① ② ③ ④ ⑤
① ② ③ ④ ⑤	17. We collect needs at all three levels of planning: strategic, tactical, and operational.	① ② ③ ④ ⑤
	18. When we do strategic planning, we formally consider and collect data for the following Ideal Vision purposes:	
① ② ③ ④ ⑤	a) There will be no losses of life or elimination or reduction of levels of well-being, survival, self-sufficiency, or quality of life from any source.	① ② ③ ④ ⑤
① ② ③ ④ ⑤	b) Eliminate terrorism, illegal civil protest, war, and/or riot.	① ② ③ ④ ⑤
① ② ③ ④ ⑤	c) Eliminate unintended human-caused changes to the environment including permanent destruction of the environment and/or rendering it nonrenewable.	① ② ③ ④ ⑤
① ② ③ ④ ⑤	d) Eliminate murder, rape, or crimes of violence, robbery, or destruction of property.	① ② ③ ④ ⑤
① ② ③ ④ ⑤	e) Eliminate disabling substance abuse.	① ② ③ ④ ⑤
① ② ③ ④ ⑤	f) Eliminate disabling diseases.	① ② ③ ④ ⑤
① ② ③ ④ ⑤	g) Eliminate starvation and/or malnutrition.	① ② ③ ④ ⑤

(continued)

The Manager's Pocket Guide to Mega Thinking and Planning

Respond to each item below using the following scale. Use this scale for both **What Is** and **What Should Be**.

    1 – Rarely, if ever   4 – Frequently
    2 – Not usually   5 – Consistently
    3 – Sometimes

WHAT IS	STRATEGIC THINKING AND PLANNING SURVEY	WHAT SHOULD BE
① ② ③ ④ ⑤	19. The elements of the Ideal Vision (a through g above) are treated as interrelated, not just each one independently.	① ② ③ ④ ⑤
① ② ③ ④ ⑤	20. Planning is done before taking action.	① ② ③ ④ ⑤
① ② ③ ④ ⑤	21. Plans are used when making decisions.	① ② ③ ④ ⑤

Table 1.1 Defining What Is and What Should Be for gaining commitment to Mega Thinking and Planning.

Do you notice any gaps that you might want to close in order to be successful? At the end of the book, this exercise will be repeated so that you can calibrate your change.

Define Success Using Mega Thinking and Planning

Action Steps

1. Consider that whatever you do, you are dealing with change, choices, and consequences. Put that to work for you.
2. Always ask and answer "if my organization is the solution, what's the problem?"
3. Master and constantly apply the three guides for delivering success:
   - the Organizational Elements Model
   - the Ideal Vision
   - the Six Critical Success Factors
4. Use the assessment instrument in Table 1.1 to identify the gaps between What Is in your organization and What Should Be for Mega Thinking and Planning. This can be done with others in your organization to obtain common understanding and commitment to useful strategic thinking and planning.

Endnotes

1. Moore, S. (2010). *Ethics by design: Strategic thinking and planning for exemplary performance, responsible results, and societal accountability.* Amherst, MA: HRD Press, Inc.

2. *Mega Planning* is a form of strategic planning. Strategic thinking is how one goes about creating a Mega plan based on adding measurable value to both the organization and society. Strategic planning is formulating a blueprint of where an organization should head based on adding measurable value within and external to one's own organization. From this point on, when we say *Mega Planning*, it should be noted that it includes strategic thinking and planning.

3. Increasing attention is being paid by "mainstream" organizations to societal value added that goes beyond building playgrounds or collecting money for charities:

   Bernardez, M. (2005). Achieving business success by developing clients and community: Lessons from leading companies, emerging economies, and a nine-year case study. *Performance Improvement Quarterly, 18*(3), pp. 37–55.

   Bernardez, M. (2008). *Capital intellectual.* Bloomington, IN: AuthorHouse.

   Bernardez, M. (May–June, 2009). Sailing the winds of "creative destruction": Educational technology during economic downturns. *Educational Technology, 22*(2), pp. 17–72.

   Bernardez, M. (2009). Minding the business of business: Tools and models to design and measure wealth creation. *Performance Improvement Quarterly, 22*(2), pp. 17–72.

   Davis, I. (May 26, 2005). The biggest contract. *The Economist.* London, Vol. 375, Iss. 8428, p. 87.

   Drucker, P. F. (Sept.–Oct., 1992). The new society of organizations. *Harvard Business Review, 70*(5), pp. 95–104.

Garratt, B. (2005). Can boards of directors think strategically? Some issues in developing direction-givers' thinking to a Mega level. *Performance Improvement Quarterly, 18*(3), pp. 26–36.

Guerra-Lopez, I. (2007). *Evaluating impact: Evaluation and continual improvement for performance improvement practitioners.* Amherst, MA: HRD Press, Inc.

Kaufman, R. (Jan 28, 2010). Should we have to wait for a crisis in order to transform public sector organizations? *Leader to Leader:* Peter F. Drucker Foundation Newsletter.

Kaufman, R., & Guerra-Lopez, I. (2008). *The assessment book: Applied strategic thinking and performance improvement through self-assessments.* Amherst, MA: HRD Press, Inc.

Kaufman, R., Oakley-Browne, H., Watkins, R., & Leigh, D. (2003). *Practical strategic planning: Aligning people, performance, and payoffs.* San Francisco, CA: Jossey-Bass/Pfeiffer.

4. Carleton, R. (2010). *Implementation and management of performance improvement plans: Emphasizing group & organizational interventions.* Amherst, MA: HRD Press, Inc. Especially Chapter 3.

5. This book has a primary focus on organizations, both public and private. The concepts and tools provided here can also be applied to personal and family life:

Kaufman, R. (2006). *30 Seconds that can change your life: A decision-making guide for those who refuse to be mediocre.* Amherst, MA: HRD Press, Inc.

6. From Kaufman, R., & Guerra-Lopez, I. (2008). *The assessment book: Applied strategic thinking and performance improvement through self-assessments.* Amherst, MA: HRD Press, Inc.

Chapter 2

The Organizational Elements Model: Ensuring that We Work at the Correct Level

The first guide for successful Mega Thinking and Planning identifies the various organizational levels that have to be linked and aligned, just as all parts of your body are essential and they have to work with all other parts of your body.

Guide One: The Organizational Elements Model (OEM)[1]

The Organizational Elements—what an organization uses, does, produces, delivers, and the external contributions—help avoid splintering and fragmentation. For any initiative, look at both the whole as well as the parts. Ensure that each of the organizational elements *Mega, Macro,* and *Micro* as well as *Processes* and *Inputs* are considered rigorously and correctly. This ensures that they are all aligned one with the others so that what any organization uses, does, produces, and delivers outside of itself adds value to our shared world. See Figure 2.1 for a list of questions each organization must ask and answer.

> - Do you commit to deliver organizational contributions that add value for society? (MEGA)
> - Do you commit to deliver organizational contributions that have the quality required by your external partners? (MACRO)
> - Do you commit to produce internal results that have the quality required by your internal partners? (MICRO)
> - Do you commit to have efficient internal processes, programs, projects, and activities? (PROCESSES)
> - Do you commit to create and ensure the quality and appropriateness of the human, capital, and physical resources available? (INPUTS)
> - Do you commit to deliver (a) products, activities, methods and procedures that have positive value and worth? (b) the results and accomplishments defined by our objectives? (EVALUATION/CONTINUAL IMPROVEMENT)

Figure 2.1. The Organizational Elements Model (OEM) stated in terms of the questions each organization must ask and answer.

Mega is about adding value to society and external clients, Macro is about what an organization delivers outside of itself, and Micro is about contributions made by individuals and small groups within the organization.

Ask yourself (and those you work with) "Which one of the organizational elements do you think we can afford to *not* deal with precisely, rigorously, and measurably?" Most will agree that all Organizational Elements are important and must be included and addressed rigorously and measurably and should be linked.

Ensure that each element will deliver results that add up with all others—add value to all internal and external stakeholders. Simply focusing on only one or two of the elements will likely result in failure. After all, we all live in a world where we and our

The Organizational Elements Model

organizations are nothing more (or nothing less) than means to societal ends.

Each of the Organizational Elements will yield performance data, and taken together, they will provide the "vital signs" of your organization. Using them will give you an "organizational check-up" similar to the annual check-up you would get from your family physician.

The Organizational Elements must be linked and aligned. Doing so ensures that everything you use (Inputs) and do (Processes) as well as individual results (Micro) and organizational contributions (Outputs) deliver useful societal results (Mega); all in the value chain are both served well and well served. Figure 2.2 shows how the elements link and align.

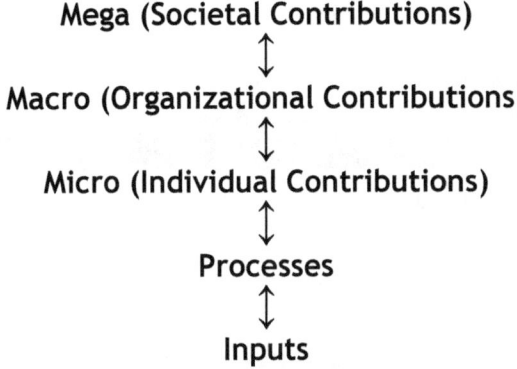

Figure 2.2. The Organizational Elements Model (OEM) and how the Organizational Elements link and align so that each adds value to all levels.

Some examples for each element of planning and each type of result for each level are included in Figure 2.3.

Mega

- Everyone is self-sufficient and self-reliant—not under the care, custody, or control of another person, agency, or substance
- Organizations (including clients and customers) are successful over time[2]
- Eliminated disabling illness due to environmental pollution
- Eliminated disabling fatalities
- Positive quality of life
- No welfare recipients (and thus their consumption is less than their production)
- Zero disabling crime
- Continued profit over time (5 years and beyond)
- Created jobs that add value over time
- Clients' success over time (5 years and beyond)
- School completer is self-sufficient and self-reliant

Macro

- Assembled automobiles
- Goods and/or services sold
- System delivered
- Patient discharged
- High school graduate

Micro

- Tire
- Fender
- Production quota met
- Completed carpet production batch
- Completed training manuals
- Competent worker
- Course completed
- Operational completed
- Test or course passed

(continued)

The Organizational Elements Model

Processes

- Organizational development
- Management techniques
- Operating production line
- 360° feedback
- Training
- Six Sigma
- Curriculum
- Examining patient
- Strategic (or tactical or operational) planning
- Assessing needs
- Course development

Inputs

- Money
- People
- Equipment
- Facilities
- Existing goals
- Existing policies
- Time
- Resources
- Individual values
- Laws
- Current economic conditions
- Regulations
- History
- Organizational culture
- Current problems
- Existing materials
- Current staff and their skills, knowledge, attitudes, and abilities
- Characteristics of current and potential clients
- Predicted client desires and requirements

Figure 2.3. Examples for each of the Organizational Elements.

For each organizational element, there is an associated level of planning: strategic planning (and thinking) starts with Mega (societal value-added) while tactical planning starts with Macro (organizational contributions) and operational planning with Micro contributions from individuals and small groups (Table 2.1).[3]

Organizational Element: MEGA		
Brief Description and Level of focus	Type of Planning	Type of Result
The results and their consequences for external clients and society (based on a shared Ideal Vision)	Strategic	Outcome
Organizational Element: MACRO		
The results and their consequences for what an organization can or does deliver outside of itself	Tactical	Output
Organizational Element: MICRO		
The results and their consequences for individuals and small groups within the organization	Operational	Product
Organizational Element: PROCESS		
Means, programs, projects, activities, methods, techniques		
Organizational Element: INPUT		
Human, capital, and physical resources, existing rules, regulations, policies, laws, existing organizational structure		

Table 2.1. Three levels of results, the label for each type of results, and the planning focus for each[4].

The Organizational Elements Model

Defining *strategic* as adding value to society and *tactical* as defining the best ways and means to deliver societal results is pragmatic. Differentiating among types of planning and results prevents the blurring of the three different levels of planning: Mega/Societal, Macro/Organizational, and Micro/Individual and encourages planners to justify any organizational mission in terms of Mega. These elements are also useful for defining the basic questions every organization must ask and answer.

Putting the OEM to work. To locate what you are doing and to make sure that you realize that each of the elements are equally important as well as linked with all the others, simply ask yourself, "At what Organizational Element is this?" Remember, just because something is big or really important doesn't make it Mega.

Try the exercise in Figure 2.4 for a pizza manufacturer so that you can target an initiative or condition to the OEM and locate it in the entire OEM context. Read each condition, then place a check under the Organizational Element you feel pertains to the condition.

Condition	Mega	Macro	Micro	Process	Input
There are 27 new employees this month.					
Last year, 4 people died from food poisoning caused by this item.					
Our company shipped 437,309 frozen pizzas last month.					
Training and mentoring are being provided monthly.					
The rejection-rate on the line last month was 9%.					
We use team management in this plant.					
New ovens arrive in October.					
Production overall is up 7%.					

(continued)

Check your answers:

Condition	Mega	Macro	Micro	Process	Input
There are 27 new employees this month.					✓
Last year, 4 people died from food poisoning caused by this item.	✓				
Our company shipped 437,309 frozen pizzas last month.		✓			
Training and mentoring are being provided monthly.				✓	
The rejection-rate on the line last month was 9%.			✓		
We use team management in this plant.				✓	
New ovens arrive in October.					✓
Production overall is up 7%.			✓		

Figure 2.4. A basis for a dialog about commitment to adding value to all internal and external stakeholders.

Defining, justifying, designing, and delivering useful organizational results are possible. They only require you to choose and use those concepts and tools that will help you select appropriate actions that will deliver measurable success.

What you use, do, produce, and deliver must all align to add value—measurable value—to your organization's internal and external partners. And that is what is almost always missing in other approaches: adding measurable value to yourself and all stakeholders. Most other approaches start and stop with the immediate bottom line and do not ensure that everyone wins. Winning requires leaving something "on the table" for everyone. Short-term greed leads to long-term failure. Not attending to external and societal consequences was central to most failures in

The Organizational Elements Model

business and government we noted earlier.[5] Be sure to link and align Mega, Macro, and Micro with the Processes and Inputs. Think Mega, think holistically. It will pay striking dividends.

Choices and making decisions. The practical choice is that there must be a partnership that seeks success for all stakeholders both within and outside of the organization—by design and by intention. The focus on societal value added—*Mega* level—is also ethical[6]...if we are not adding value to society, we are subtracting value.[7]

Decisions (and not making a decision is a decision) can be made easier and more effective if we consider the consequences of simply doing what we are now doing or deciding to change in order to get different rewards or payoffs. If you want to have a different life (including your personal one as well as your organization), simply do what it takes to get different results and consequences.

Figure 2.5 provides a guide to making decisions that will be both successful and satisfying.

Basic Decision-Making Steps
(based on Greenwald)[8]

- Identify the payoffs you are getting now that you don't want.
- Identify the behaviors you are now displaying that deliver the negative payoff.
- Identify the payoffs you do want.
- Identify the behaviors and actions that will deliver the desired payoffs.
- Decide to change your behavior.
- Change.
- Be ready to decide to change in the future if you want different payoffs.

Figure 2.5. The steps of decision making.

When we talk about decisions and changes, think of these basic steps and include Mega in your list of payoffs, payoffs being the rewards and consequences of our decisions. If you want to change what is happening to you, in an organization, or in life[9] to something positive, these steps will be of great value. Of course, staying objective and complete is essential.

Your success will be better assured if you make decisions based on using all the Organizational Elements. Not doing so is very risky.

Action Steps

1. Use the Organizational Elements Model (OEM)—Mega, Macro, Micro, Processes, and Inputs—to serve you:

   - Identify the three levels of results and two levels of activities and resources.

   - Allow you to identify any considered action, procedure, initiative, or change and where it is in the total value chain of the OEM. Let it keep you from selecting solutions before knowing the problems.

   - Use the OEM to serve as a guide to achieve agreement among your internal and external partners of what should be used, done, produced, delivered, and the value it will add for all stakeholders.

2. Differentiate among Strategic (Mega), Tactical (Macro), and Operational (Micro) planning, and ensure that all levels of planning and results are linked and aligned to ensure success.

3. Use words clearly and with precise meaning. That will help you work with others and not confuse terms and what you have to design and deliver.

4. Complete a dialog with others and get the required commitment to Mega thinking and planning. Figure 2.4 will help.

(continued)

The Organizational Elements Model

> 5. Not making a decision is a decision. A useful decision guide, based on Greenwald, is presented in Figure 2.5.
>
> 6. Be clear with yourself and others and continue to think and act Mega.

Endnotes

1. This is not the same as Original Equipment Manufacturer that is used in some industries, although we rely on them to focus on Mega as primary.

2. The words "over time" are critical. Success over time indicates that what it delivers to external clients is safe and useful and that is also reflected in continuing profits and no successful liability lawsuits against them.

3. Note that these definitions of *strategic* and *tactical* are different from other conventional usages.

4. Kaufman, R. (2006). *Change, choices, and consequences: A guide to Mega Thinking and Planning.* Amherst, MA: HRD Press, Inc.

5. A major contribution is the two-level business case created by Dr. Mariano Bernardez. His approach, the inclusion of Mega as well as Macro, allows us to see the true costs and consequences of including societal value added:

   Bernardez, M. (2009). Minding the business of business: Tools and models to design and measure wealth creation. *Performance Improvement Quarterly, 22*(2), pp. 17–72.

6. Moore, S. (2010). *Ethics by design: Strategic thinking and planning for exemplary performance, responsible results, and societal accountability.* Amherst, MA: HRD Press, Inc.

7. Brethower, D. (2006). *Performance analysis: Knowing what to do and how.* Amherst, MA: HRD Press, Inc.

8. Greenwald, H. (1973). *Decision Therapy.* NY: Peter Wyden, Inc.
9. Guidance on applying Mega to one's own life is in Kaufman, R. (2006). *30 Seconds that can change your life: A decision-making guide for those who refuse to be mediocre.* Amherst, MA: HRD Press, Inc.

Chapter 3

The Ideal Vision: Selecting Where You Are Headed and Justifying Why You Want to Get There

It makes good sense to ensure that where you and your organization are headed is where you should be headed. Most organizations are not clear about their purpose, and, as Bob Mager, the outstanding expert on objectives tells us, if we don't know where we are going, we might end up someplace else.[1] The *Ideal Vision* will provide you and your organization with clear, justifiable, and specific criteria for choosing your purpose: where you are headed and how to tell when you have arrived.

Organizations today are awash in labels about their purpose: "visions," "missions," "goals," and "purposes." Most are often silly (for example, what does "world-class" mean and how would you measure it?) and are rarely precise and rigorous enough for you to actually plan to get there.[2] That does not have to be the case, and you can choose to make sure that everyone agrees on where you are headed and why you want to get there.

It is useful to get everyone to agree on a common destination before they, individually and uniquely, contribute in their own way in their own domain to deliver the agreed-upon results. Guide 2 provides just that.

Guide 2. The Ideal Vision as a Practical and Agreed-Upon Statement of Shared Destinations for You and Your Organization

Successful strategic planning and strategic thinking—creating your future—are based in defining where to go and justifying why you want to get there. The basis for "where to go" and "why get there" resides in a simple but often overlooked reality: we all are means to societal ends. You, me, our organizations are all means to societal ends. When we think strategically, we focus on adding value to our shared society, and then we plan strategically to get measurable societal results.

Society, Mega, and the rational choice. The basic rational choice is to make external clients and society—Mega—the planning frame. When you do, it is the safest, most practical, and ethical choice. When we choose our external clients and our shared society (Mega-level thinking and planning) as our planning frame, we can then sensibly align our workgroups and our organization to add value as we move from internal contributions to external ones.[3] This guiding principle is simple and straightforward, and it makes intuitive sense.

From this shared societal value-added frame,[4] everything you and your organization uses, does, produces, and delivers is linked to achieve shared and agreed-upon positive societal results. Using this common definition of "societal good" for your organization will allow you to derive your Mission Objective from it in terms of those elements that you commit to deliver and move ever-closer toward. This common agreement on the mission (based on the elements of Mega) will allow each individual, group, department, and division in your organization to design their contributions to that shared destination. Doing so will reduce internal competition and effectively allow each to make their unique contributions.

While most planning participants look to see if their area of interest is included in the mission objective, does so will make the mission weaker by including such means as "quality assurance," or "non-discriminatory behavior," or "integrated teams," or in an academic environment "arts and performing arts." This can be handled if you add a section below the Mission Objective labeled "possible implementation vehicles." There such treasured vehicles and interests can be listed and then considered when solutions and activities are decided.

Mega thinking—your mind set, or frame of reference based on adding value to our shared communities and society—is guided by an *Ideal Vision*[5] that is in Figure 3.1. Note that the label *Ideal Vision* is just that, ideal. It is that shared "North Star" toward which you and all others steer and combine your contributions to get from here to there.

We might not get there in our lifetime or the lifetime of our children, but if that is not where we are headed, where do we

The Ideal Vision

head? The definition of an Ideal Vision in Figure 3.1—yes, this is ideal only and sets the destination toward which we should continually move—that has been derived from asking people from around most of the world, "What kind of world do you want to help create for tomorrow's child?"

> **Basic Ideal Vision**
>
> The world we want to help create—with others—for tomorrow's child.
>
> There will be no losses of life nor elimination or reduction of levels of survival, self-sufficiency, or quality of life from any source including (but not limited to) the following:
>
> - war, riot, terrorism, or unlawful civil unrest
> - unintended human-caused changes to the environment (including permanent destruction of the environment and/or rendering it nonrenewable)
> - murder, rape, or crimes of violence, robbery, or destruction to property
> - substance abuse
> - permanent or continuing disabilities
> - disease
> - starvation and/or malnutrition
> - destructive behavior including child, partner, spouse, self, elder, others
> - accidents, including transportation, home, and business/workplace
> - discrimination based on irrelevant variables (including color, race, age, creed, gender, religion, wealth, national origin, or location)

(continued)

> **Consequences:** Poverty will not exist, and every woman and man will earn at least as much as it costs them to live unless they are progressing toward being self-sufficient and self-reliant. No adult will be under the care, custody, or control of another person, agency, or substance: all adult citizens will be self-sufficient and self-reliant as minimally indicated by their consumption being equal to or less than their production.

Figure 3.1. An Ideal Vision: It states in measurable terms the kind of world—an ideal world—we want to, together, create for tomorrow's child.[6]

Why does using Mega make sense? It builds on the reality that what we use, do, produce, and deliver should build a better world—a world we want to help create for tomorrow's child. It is rational if for no other reason that we all depend on each other for contributing to our safety, survival, and well-being and all others should be able to depend on us for the same. Thinking and planning Mega, however, is a choice, and like all other choices, you are responsible for the consequences of them.[7]

Using the Ideal Vision will allow you to answer the central question that each and every organization should ask and answer posed in Chapter 1: If my organization is the solution, what's the problem?

Asking and answering this question require clearly noting that your organization should have a role in assisting everyone to survive, be self-sufficient and self-reliant, and have a positive quality of life; our organization should add societal value.

This proposition is central to Mega Thinking and Planning strategically and firmly puts everyone on notice that your organization must contribute to external and societal (Mega) contributions. It represents a shift from the usual focus only on oneself, individual performance improvement, and one's organization to making certain you also add value to external clients and society. In working with your organization, ask the question: "If my organization is the solution, what's the problem?" The dialog that

The Ideal Vision

will result usually lets people know that they and the organization are only a means to societal ends. If the organization is not adding measurable value to external clients and society, it is at serious risk.

Conventionally, most organizations stop at what is immediately good for them and their organization (the so-called bottom line or standard business case) and neglect to make sure they and their organization are also adding value outside of themselves. Some organizations don the cloak of Corporate Social Responsibility (CSR) and dodge their central Mega-level responsibility to add value to our shared society by such cosmetic responses as building swings for playgrounds, "1% days" where that percentage of all sales go to charity, or working in the community. These are useful but no substitute for ensuring that everything the organizations deliver outside of their organization will add value to all stakeholders.

One example of Mega is United Parcel Service (UPS) that does both community as well as charity outreach. In the performance of their organization worldwide, they set objectives and use hard performance indicators to track environmental and safety contributions as well.[8] This is but one example of an increasing number of organizations adding value to both shareholders as well as to communities. More examples are in Chapter 9.

Table 3.1 has an exercise for you and your associates to use to commit to which of the Organizational Elements they will address formally, precisely, and rigorously.

Basic Ideal Vision Elements

There will be no loss of life or elimination of the survival of any species required for human survival. There will be no reductions in levels of self-sufficiency, quality of life, livelihood, or loss of property from any source, including:	Makes a Contribution:		
	Directly	Indirectly	None
war, riot, terrorism, or unlawful civil unrest			
shelter			
unintended human-caused changes to the environment, including permanent destruction of the environment and/or rendering it nonrenewable			
murder, rape, or crimes of violence, robbery, or destruction to property			
substance abuse			
disease			
pollution			
starvation and/or malnutrition			
child abuse			
partner/spouse abuse			
accidents, including transportation, home, and business/workplace			
discrimination based on irrelevant variables, including color, race, creed, sex, religion, national origin, age, location			
Poverty will not exist, and every woman and man will earn at least as much as it costs them to live unless they are progressing toward being self-sufficient and self-reliant			
No adult will be under the care, custody, or control of another person, agency, or substance; all adult citizens will be self-sufficient and self-reliant as minimally indicated by their consumption being equal to or less than their production			

(continued)

The Ideal Vision

> **Consequences of the Basic Ideal Vision:**
>
> Any and all organizations—public and private—will contribute to the achievement and maintenance of this Basic Ideal Vision and will be funded and continued to the extent to which it meets its objectives and the Basic Ideal Vision is accomplished and maintained.
>
> People will be responsible for what they use, do, and contribute and thus will not contribute to the reduction of any of the results identified in this Basic Ideal Vision.

Table 3.1. An exercise to select which elements of the Ideal Vision you and your organization commit to deliver and move ever-closer toward.

Contributing to societal good is not a passing gimmick.

Attention on and direct contribution to our shared society seem to be growing. Making money and doing societal good must not be mutually exclusive.

The use of the label *Corporate Social Responsibility (CSR)* might signal a growing interest in societal consequences. Even the worldwide managing director of McKinsey & Company, Ian Davis, has noted the "biggest contact" for every organization is societal good and notes that it is central to strategic planning, not an adjunct to it.[9] This shift is especially important if one only uses the conventional approach to only looking at last quarter's financial results as the only measure of success. Just looking after the bottom line is no longer enough. Viable CSR should include rigorous indicators of measurable societal value added to its scorecard, not just tinkering with some of the possible elements of adding social value.

Sensibly and happily, organizations are joining the movement that adding societal value is not only necessary ethically but makes good business sense. The business of business is business if it also adds value to our shared world at the same time. Increasing examples of measurable results from thinking and acting Mega are now finding their way into publication.[10] This represents a shift away from the usual and aging concept that the business sole focus on the bottom line may be giving way to an additional and primary focus on Mega thinking and planning.[11] Adding societal value and using your talents and your organization's is practical, smart, ethical, and safe.

Justifying Mega from literature. Turning to a literary source for not thinking, planning, and doing what is conventional—assuming that what has worked in the past will work in the future—is Macbeth:

> To-morrow, and to-morrow, and to-morrow,
> Creeps in this petty pace from day to day
> To the last syllable of recorded time,
> **And all our yesterdays have lighted fools**
> **The way to dusty death.** Out, out, brief candle!
> Life's but a walking shadow, a poor player
> That struts and frets his hour upon the stage
> And then is heard no more: it is a tale
> Told by an idiot, full of sound and fury,
> Signifying nothing. (Macbeth, Act 5, Scene 5, emphasis added)

The insight nested in this classic soliloquy is that simply building on all that has gone before us might not be the way to go—and may even be disastrous.

The hallmark of the Mega approach to strategic planning and thinking suggested in this book is a focus on society and using yourself and your organization as the vehicle for adding value. In considering this, here are two questions:

- What are the risks for not thinking, planning, and doing Mega?
- What are the risks for thinking, planning, and doing Mega?

Mega Results for Individuals, Organizations, and Society: Measuring Consequences

Measurement is both vital and tricky. How do we know when someone is self-sufficient and self-reliant? When can we tell when they are not under the care, custody, or control of another person, substance, or agency? Good questions, and ones for which we should have answers.

The Ideal Vision

In the Ideal Vision (Figure 3.1), we note that each individual should at least be self-sufficient and self-reliant. How can we tell?

One useful indicator is that a person's consumption (what she pays for) is equal to or less than their production (what they get paid for).[12] A simple equation is

$$C \leq P$$

where C is consumption (in monies paid out) and P is production (for which one gets income). This is an indicator of self-sufficiency and self-reliance.

Additional indicators might be used for individuals:

- making more than you spend
- not in jail
- not on government transfer payments (e.g., welfare, relief, food stamps, charity)
- positive credit rating
- not in a mental institution
- not homeless
- not under the care, custody, or control of another person, substance, or agency

Is all of this a bit mercenary? Perhaps at first light, but it really is practical and pragmatic.

No matter the culture, there is always some token of exchange, be it in pounds, Yuen, dollars, Euros, shells, or cattle. We keep track in terms of some form of money. Does such an indicator cover all possible criteria or does this give a perfect fit with actual survival, self-sufficiency, and quality of life? No, but at least it provides some metrics for us to use and improve.

The use of societal value-added criteria by applying $C \leq P$ was used in the State of Florida to determine the basic value of several Job Training Partnership programs that were intended to improve employability and remove them from public assistance.[13] When examined using the conventional criteria of completion of training and job placement as well as the societal return-on-investment, it was found that two of the three programs showed both increased wages and increased employment, while one program did not have a significant positive return-on-investment.

The approach of including Mega—societal value-added—allowed decision makers to continue what was working and revise that which was not performing up to fiscal responsibility.

Data exist concerning Mega as more and more professionals and managers recognize including societal costs and consequences. For example (Figure 3.2), research on what Deming called the "costs of non-quality" bad behavior shows some impact criteria for calculating the costs and consequences of Mega-related variables:[14]

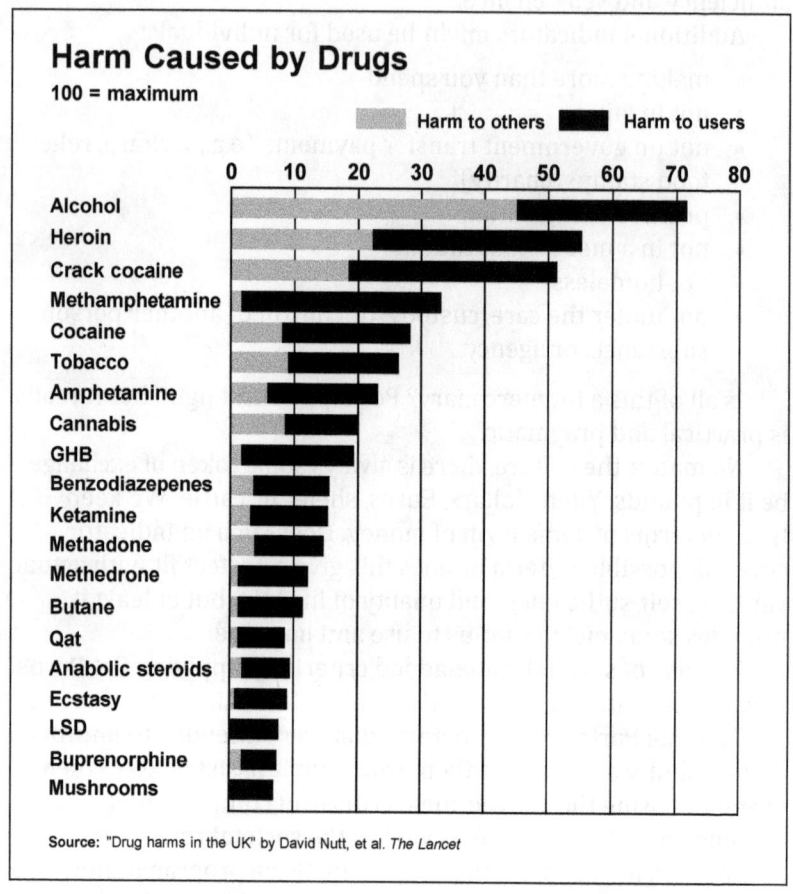

Figure 3.2. Some data on the Mega-related costs of "non-quality" that can be considered in Mega planning.[15]

The Bernardez 2-Level Business Case Model

A unique, yet powerful application business case model has been developed by Bernardez[16] and has been applied successfully in both the public and private sectors. He has created and validated a unique and powerful 2-level business case model. The model collects and applies metrics for both the elements of a conventional bottom line for an organization (e.g., profit, jobs) and links that with a societal (Mega) bottom. In this approach, Micro—individual performance contributions—are included. Table 3.2 provides an example for an incubator business organization associated with a Mexican University. It shows how Mega and Macro and Micro results can be computed to show a conventional as well as a societal (Mega) return-on-investment:

Business Intelligence Center (Trans Pacific)

U.S. DOLLARS

MEGA "TOP LINE"	2007-2011	2007	2008	2009	2010	2011
Direct jobs	90	10	15	20	20	25
Ratio indirect jobs/direct jobs		0.5	0.5	0.5	0.4	0.4
Indirect job as	200	20	30	40	50	60
Annual average income direct jobs	5,362	5,365	5,368	5,371	5,374	5,377
Annual average income indirect jobs	5,362	5,365	5,368	5,371	5,374	5,377
Direct jobs "ripple effect" revenue	483,495	53,650	80,520	107,420	107,480	134,425
Indirect jobs "ripple effect" revenue	1,074,500	107,300	161,040	214,840	268,700	322,620
Tax revenue for state and community	303	9,090	13,635	18,180	21,210	25,755
Exports revenue	47,019		10,909	11,454	12,027	12,629
MEGA RESULTS	**1,605,014**	**170,040**	**266,104**	**351,894**	**409,417**	**495,429**

(continued)

The Ideal Vision

MACRO "TOP LINE"	2007-2011	2007	2008	2009	2010	2011
Products and Services Revenue						
Research		3,600	4,200	4,800	5,400	6,000
Business plans		3,000	3,500	4,000	4,500	5,000
Special projects		2,500	3,750	3,750	6,250	7,500
Stages and exchange						
Other ITSON services (non BIC programs)		10,022	13,559	21,232	29,850	30,669
MACRO RESULTS	**173,082**	**19,122**	**25,009**	**33,782**	**46,000**	**49,169**
DOUBLE TOP LINE (MEGA + MACRO)	**1,778,096**	**189,162**	**291,113**	**385,676**	**455,417**	**544,598**
MICRO	2007-2011	2007	2008	2009	2010	2011
Products and Services Delivered						
Research	80	12	14	16	18	20
Business plans	80	12	14	16	18	20
Special projects	95	10	15	15	25	30
Stages and exchange	10	2	2	2	2	2
Other ITSON products and services	**300**	**40**	**50**	**60**	**70**	**80**
TOTAL MICRO OUTPUT	**565**	**76**	**95**	**109**	**133**	**152**

(continued)

COST	2007-2011	2007	2008	2009	2010	2011
Initial investment	45,454	45,454				
Non-ITSON financial support	1,500	1,500	1,500	1,500	1,500	1,500
Licenses	1,000	1,000				
IT equipment	2,000	2,000				
Operational costs		3,600	3,602	3,604	3,606	3,608
Stages and exchanges	2,250	4,500	4,500	4,500	4,500	4,500
TOTAL COST	90,474	58,054	8,102	8,104	8,106	8,108
CONVENTIONAL BOTTOM LINE		-58,054	-41,147	-32,376	-20,160	-16,993
DOUBLE BOTTOM LINE		131,108	181,060	283,009	377,570	447,309
CONVENTIONAL ROI (MACRO/COST)		-1.28	-0.91	-0.71	-0.44	-0.37
SOCIAL ROI (MEGA + MACRO/COST)		2.88	3.98	6.23	8.31	9.84

Table 3.2. An example of an application of Bernardez's 2-level business case.

The Ideal Vision

To prove success and value added for your planning, this model can be used "before the fact" to project returns and "after the fact" to prove ultimate value and return. In the example in Table 3.2, the ratio of conventional return-on-investment and the one for social (Mega) return-on-investment are shown so that a rational decision can be made on the basis of feasibility of including the Mega consequences.

Another of a large-scale application was a two-level business case done for the leadership and cabinet of Panama, where it was applied to show the costs and consequences of transforming a major city from disrepair, crime, and poverty to put it on a par with the country's successful metropolis. The application of the Bernardez model provided the president and cabinet with a strategic option so that Colon City could be transformed, including buildings, infrastructure, and all aspects of the city, and that there would be a positive return-on-investment within the first year.[17]

For more limited estimates of value added. If one is only interested in costing-out training and only to the level of profit-and-loss for an organization but not including societal value-added, Phillips[18] provides some guidelines. Of course, adding societal impact and consequences are basic to Mega thinking and planning.

These ways of measuring progress and success will be revisited in Chapter 8, Implementing the Mega Plan.

What if my boss or my associates are not ready for Mega?
They might not be at first. You may help them to see the wisdom in their making better choices. And recent concerns in mainstream business as well as public sector organizations (both in the United States and abroad) show that a primary focus on societal value added is evolving.

But you can "educate" others, including a boss. You can help them see the benefits of thinking and planning Mega as compared to the costs for not doing so. If they don't want to add value to their clients and the shared communities and society in which we all live, what do they have in mind? Who will be called to account for not adding measurable value to all stakeholders? Will they be able to defend their decisions in the harsh light of publicity?

When there is initial resistance, it is often about fear: fear of not knowing how to add societal value, fear that no one else is now doing that, or fear that they don't have enough control over what gets used, done, produced, and delivered in terms of the impact all of that has on both the bottom line and consequences for our world.

One possibility for not "seeing" the importance of a Mega focus is saliency—how important it is to a person. If one doesn't see that survival and self-sufficiency is not staring them in the eye—no immediacy—they might defer doing anything about Mega. The closer one is to the survival lever (such as when in a war, or facing a devastating health situation, impending natural disaster, imminent threat), the more Mega seems important. To deal with possible denial is to help people see the real links between what they use, do, produce, and deliver and measurable societal consequences. When given the cool and rational opportunity to consider their choices—organizational alone or organizational + external clients and society—most make the practical choice.

To help, see the decision guide in Table 1.1 for working with others to get agreement on Mega: it provides a self-check that you and others in your organization can use to reinforce the choice of Mega, using the Ideal Vision for performance indicators, for your individual and organizational success.

Undecided? To paraphrase President John F. Kennedy in his inaugural address: *If not now, when? If not us, who?*

The Ideal Vision

Action Steps

1. Use the Ideal Vision as the basis for everything you and your organization uses, does, produces, and delivers to our shared society.

2. Realize that Mega is the rational, practical, and ethical choice.

3. Get commitment to the Ideal Vision and identify those elements that you and your organization now target and will continue to target and deliver. Table 3.1 and Figure 2.4 will be useful.

4. Measure value added for each initiative, program, project, or activity. There are several that you may use, including $C \leq P$. Also, of major value is the Bernardez 2-level business case that can demonstrate conventional bottom-line results (Macro) and societal bottom-line results (Mega).

Endnotes

1. Mager, R. F. (1997). *Preparing instructional objectives: A critical tool in the development of effective instruction.* (3rd ed.). Atlanta, GA: Center for Effective Performance.

2. c.f. Kaufman, R., Stith, M., & Kaufman, J. D. (Feb. 1992). Extending performance technology to improve strategic market planning. *Performance & Instruction Journal, 31*(2), pp. 38–43.

3. Table 2.1 shows the three levels of planning and results.

4. The process for defining and using Mega relies on the democratic process of all persons who could be impacted by the definition of Mega coming to agreement.

5. This was derived by asking people from around the globe (not formally including Central Africa or the former Soviet Union, however) to define the world they would create for their children and grandchildren. In earlier work (Kaufman, Oakley-Browne, Watkins, & Leigh, 2003) this was also called "mother's rule" because it squares quite well when mothers, regardless of culture, are asked what kind of world they want for their children; they don't talk to means and resources but to ends and consequences related to self-sufficiency and self-reliance.

6. Based on Kaufman, 1998, 2000, 2006; Kaufman, Oakley-Browne, Watkins, & Leigh, 2003; Kaufman, Guerra, & Platt, 2006.

7. In earlier work, I called the use of Mega "practical dreaming"—a concept that management expert Wess Roberts thought appropriate enough to reference in his writings.

8. See the United Parcel Service's "sustainability report" at http://www.sustainability.ups.com/community/Static%20Files/sustainability/Highlights.pdf

The Ideal Vision

9. Ian Davis (2005) noted some of the following as sensible corporate behavior relative to strategic planning and corporate responsibility:
    - A shift away from the "create shareholder value" model to social contribution.
    - Organizations must build social issues into strategy.
    - "Social issues are not so much tangential to the business of business as fundamental to it."
    - Companies that treat social issues as either irritating distractions or simply unjustified vehicles for attacks on business are turning a blind eye to impending forces that have the potential to alter the strategic future in fundamental ways.
    - The "business of business is business" outlook obscures the requirement to address questions about their ethics and legitimacy.
    - There is an implicit contract between big business and society.
    - Business leaders have to shape the debate on social issues by establishing ever higher (but appropriate) standards of integrity and transparency.
    - Rousseau's social contract helped to seed the idea that leaders must serve the public good, lest their own legitimacy be threatened. Today's CEOs should take the opportunity to restate and reinforce their own social contracts in order to help secure, for the long terms, the invested billions of their shareholders.

    From Ian Davis, world-wide managing director of McKinsey & Company. The biggest contract. *The Economist.* London: May 28, 2005. Vol. 375, Iss. 8428, p. 87

10. Kaufman, R., & Bernardez, M. (2005). (Eds.) *Performance Improvement Quarterly.* Special invited issue on Mega planning. Volume 18, Number 3. pp. 3–5, www.ispi.org/publications/piqtocs/piq18_3.htm

    Kaufman, R., Bernardez, M., & Guerra-Lopez. (2009) Eds. *Performance Improvement Quarterly.* Special invited issue on Mega Planning. Volume 22, Number 2. www.ispi.org/publications/piqtocs/piq18_3.htm

11. I am getting less lonely since my first publication on the importance of all organizations adding measurable value to our shared society in 1969. Kaufman, R. A., Corrigan, R. E., & Johnson, D. W. (1969). Towards educational responsiveness to society's needs: A tentative utility model. *Journal of Socio-Economic Planning Sciences.* 3, pp. 151–157.

    Still, there are those who believe that the starting and endpoint of any performance improvement effort is the "business case." Until recently, the standard business case almost never formally looks at a proactive approach to adding societal value. The world is catching up concerning Mega and adding value to our shared society, as well it must. Bernardez has developed and validated a two-level business case including and linking Macro and Mega:

    Bernardez, M. (2009). Minding the business of business: Tools and models to design and measure wealth creation. *Performance Improvement Quarterly, 22*(2), pp. 17–72.

12. Muir, M., Watkins, R., Kaufman, R., & Leigh, D. (April 1998). Costs–consequences analysis: A primer. *Performance Improvement, 37*(4), pp. 8–17, 48.

    Kaufman, R., Watkins, R., Sims, L., Crispo, N., Sprague, D. (1997). Costs–consequences analysis. *Performance Improvement Quarterly. 10*(3), pp. 7–21.

13. Muir, M., Watkins, R., Kaufman, R., & Leigh, D. (April 1998). Costs–consequences analysis: A primer. *Performance Improvement, 37*(4), pp. 8–17, 48.

14. Bialik, C. (Nov. 5, 2010). That $150 pack of cigarettes. *Wall Street Journal Blog.* Bialik, C. (Nov. 6, 2010). The pitfalls of calculating bad behavior's true cost. *The New York Times.*

15. Another useful tool for documenting Mega/societal related gaps is provided at gapminderworld (gapminder.org).

16. Bernardez, M. (2009). Minding the business of business: Tools and models to design and measure wealth creation. *Performance Improvement Quarterly, 22*(2), pp. 17-72.

17. Bernardez, M., Kaufman, R., Krivatsy, A., & Arias, C. (2011). City doctors: A systemic approach to transform Colon City, Panama. *Social and Organizational Performance Review,* Vol. 3, yr. 3. The title of this article was provided by The Panamanian Minister of Tourism for his briefing to the cabinet.

18. Phillips, P. P. (2010). Converting measures into monetary value. Chapter 14 in *ASTD Handbook of Measuring and Evaluating Training.* In Phillips, P. P. (Ed.). ASTD: Arlington, VA: pp. 189-200.

Chapter 4

Six Critical Success Factors for Successful Mega Thinking and Planning

As you use Mega Thinking and Planning, there are some guidelines—critical success factors—that will help keep you on track and keep things under control.

Guide 3. Six Critical Success Factors that Apply to All Successful Organizations

The six critical success factors in Table 4.1 are basic guides (not tools) to help you ensure that what you use, do, and produce will add measurable value. Use these as you plan to make sure that everything you use, do, produce, and deliver will add measurable value.

To guide you as you create success, use the six factors for "reality checking."

> **CRITICAL SUCCESS FACTOR 1:** Don't assume that what worked in the past will work now or in the future. Get out of your comfort zone and be open to change (see Chapter 1).
>
> **CRITICAL SUCCESS FACTOR 2:** Differentiate between ends (what) and means (how) (see Chapter 5).
>
> **CRITICAL SUCCESS FACTOR 3:** Prepare all objectives—including the Ideal Vision and mission—to include measurable statements of both where you are headed as well as the criteria for measuring when you have arrived (see Chapters 5 and 6).
>
> **CRITICAL SUCCESS FACTOR 4:** Define "need" as a gap in results (not as insufficient levels of resources, means, or methods) (see Chapter 7).

(continued)

> **CRITICAL SUCCESS FACTOR 5:** Use and align all three levels of planning and results: Mega/Outcomes, Macro/Outputs, Micro/Products (see Chapter 6).
>
> **CRITICAL SUCCESS FACTOR 6:** Use an Ideal Vision (Mega: what kind of world, in measurable performance terms, we want for tomorrow's child) as the underlying basis for planning and continual improvement (see Chapter 3).

Table 4.1. Six critical success factors for Mega thinking and planning.

We have provided the basic rationale for Mega Thinking and Planning—what it is and how it can be central to your success as a manager. There are three basic considerations for defining and delivering success:

- A societal value-added "frame of mind" or paradigm: Your perspective about your organization, your people, and our world focuses on an agreed-upon approach to adding value to all stakeholders.

- A shared determination and agreement on where to head and why: All people who can and might be impacted by the shared objectives must agree on purposes and results criteria using a framework for what every organization uses, does, produces, and delivers to achieve societal value.

- Basic factors will assure you that you focus on what is important and make certain everything is on target.

These, having supplied the conceptual framework, set the stage for what is next:

> Pragmatic and basic tools for planning, design, development, implementation, and continual improvement: defining and determining the "hows" of achieving performance that is required for success

Six Critical Success Factors

To assist you, we provided the basic concepts for Mega Thinking and Planning in order to define and deliver value—measurable value—to internal and external partners. Choices should be based on rational data in order to deliver useful results. To review, the three guides to assist you in defining and delivering personal and organizational success:

Guide 1. The Organizational Elements Model (OEM) that identifies those questions that every organization must ask and answer (Figure 2.1)

Guide 2. The Ideal Vision: Agreeing on where to head and why you want to get there (Figure 3.1)

Guide 3. Six Critical Success Factors that apply to all successful organizations (Table 4.1)

It is important that you realize that as a manager and a leader, this approach is unique, practical, and proven.[1]

Table 4.2 shows a comparison of conventional "strategic" planning and the Mega Thinking and Planning approach.[2]

Traditional "Strategic" Planning	Mega Thinking and Planning Paradigm
Improve the present situation. Incremental changes to the present way of doing things.	Mega Thinking and Planning involves the design and creation of a new paradigm. It involves new concepts, realistic new rules, new techniques, and new skills to be successful. It often requires leaving the comfortable behind.
Short-term profit or funding. Objectives target only next quarter, or only a very few years in the future.	Long-term objectives that will design a better world for both today's and tomorrow's children and citizens and will make our world measurably better. Includes continual improvement. Objectives target 5 to 100^3 years plus.
A focus on tactics and activities not clearly connected to measurable organizational and external clients' results. Wants are often confused with needs.	Focuses on designing future results in measurable terms before selecting relevant tactics. Results are long-term and link all three levels: Mega, Macro, and Micro.
Objectives define financial results only. Internal clients and future citizens are largely ignored. Positive societal impact is left to chance.	Objectives are designed for a functional range of stakeholders: • 4.1 Future citizens • 4.2 Today's clients • 4.3 Internal clients • Performance indicators are chosen to evaluate success and determine revisions and changes.
Social quality is not a formal or measurable issue in planning.	Societal value-added, now and in the future, are the priority issues for planning.

(continued)

Six Critical Success Factors

"Needs" are defined as gaps in resources, methods, and means (e.g., we "need" more equipment; we "need" more computers).	"Needs" are defined as gaps between current and desired results. Requirement for more resources are quasi-needs and are only selected on the basis of the best ways and means for meeting the needs.
Level of planning focuses on immediate clients and major shareholders. Society and internal clients are not formally or rigorously considered.	Planning includes the integration and linking of three groups of clients: • 7.1 Society now and in the future • 7.2 Immediate external clients • 7.3 Internal clients
Goals are more often general, vague, and exclude measurable criteria.	Objectives are written for results at three levels, and always include measurable criteria.

Table 4.2. Comparison of conventional strategic planning and the Mega Thinking and Planning program.

This approach has a number of advantages.

1. It is holistic and doesn't artificially reduce everything down to only a part of any organization or to just a quarterly profit and loss sheet (which is, of course, an essential element but not the sole element).

2. It provides a common "North Star" for all inside and external to the organization to share and then uniquely and together contribute. This cuts down on confusion, unrequired internal competition, and delivers a unique approach and results not provided by other approaches.

3. It is results focused and builds on performance data and not on biases, stereotypes, and conventional wisdom.

4. It provides a template that identifies everything an organization uses, does, produces, and delivers, and the external value added. This can be used for considering new initiatives as well as making sure that all efforts and results are aligned and integrated toward a common and shared destination.

5. It is guided by six "rules of the road" that ensure that everything is managed to deliver useful and timely results.

Action Steps

1. Use the Six Critical Success Factors for Mega Thinking and Planning. They will guide you through decisions, commitments, and actions to define and deliver success.

2. Always think and act Mega. It will be more successful than conventional approaches.

Let's now turn to the specific tools for Mega Thinking and Planning.

Endnotes

1. Two issues of *Performance Improvement Quarterly* provide operational examples of how Mega planning works, and works well.

    Kaufman, R., & Bernardez, M. (2005). (Eds.) *Performance Improvement Quarterly* (special invited issue on Mega Planning), *18*(3), pp. 3–5.

    Kaufman, R., Bernardez, M., & Guerra-Lopez, I. (2009). (Eds.) *Performance Improvement Quarterly* (special invited issue on Mega Planning), *22*(2), pp. 17–22.

2. Based on Kaufman, R., Oakley-Browne, H., Watkins, R., & Leigh, D. (2003). *Practical strategic planning: Aligning people, performance, and payoffs.* San Francisco, CA: Jossey-Bass/Pfeiffer.

3. Several years ago on an Australian Public Radio broadcast, I was derided by one participant for setting a time frame of 5 to 25 years. However, in support, an Australian professor noted that Fuji had a 100-year planning horizon because "they intend to be in business 100 years in the future!" How long does your organization want to be in business?

Chapter 5

Objectives and Performance Specifications: The Criteria for Accomplishment[1]

Knowing where you are headed and how to accurately measure when you have arrived is central to successful planning, doing, delivering, and accomplishment; this is enabled by using *measurable objectives*. Measurable objectives are statements of where you are headed and how to measure when you have arrived; they have the performance specifications for reliably assessing completion. They also provide the criteria for planning by stating measurable results to be accomplished.

Mega Planning will additionally ensure that the "where you are headed" is the right destination. Now let's just identify how to define results—any level of result. Figure 5.1 provides some guidance.

It is vital that everything that is used, done, and delivered has data-base specifications: prepare objectives that are really useful and clearly state where you are headed and how to tell when you have arrived.

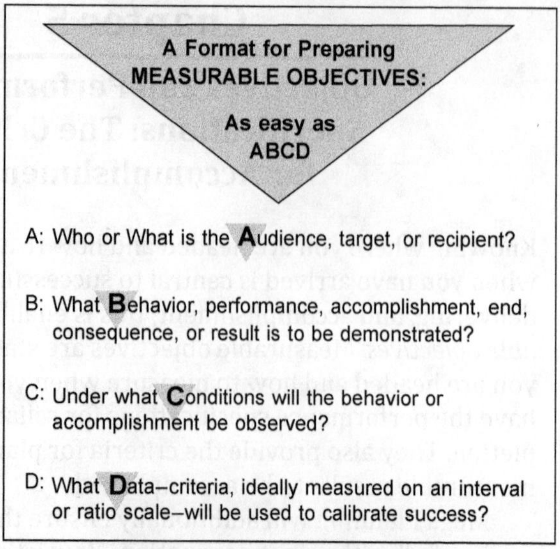

> **A Format for Preparing**
> **MEASURABLE OBJECTIVES:**
>
> **As easy as**
> **ABCD**
>
> A: Who or What is the **A**udience, target, or recipient?
>
> B: What **B**ehavior, performance, accomplishment, end, consequence, or result is to be demonstrated?
>
> C: Under what **C**onditions will the behavior or accomplishment be observed?
>
> D: What **D**ata—criteria, ideally measured on an interval or ratio scale—will be used to calibrate success?

Figure 5.1. Useful aid for formatting useful measurable objectives.

Four different scales of measurement for you to use. Because objectives should be rigorous, we can consider and use four different types of measurement. Table 5.1 identifies the four scales of measurement and the purpose of each.

Objectives and Performance Specifications

Name of Scale of Measurement	Name of Purpose They are Used For
Nominal	Goal (or Aim, or Purpose)
Ordinal	Goal (or Aim, or Purpose)
Interval	Objective
Ratio	Objective

Table 5.1. The four scales of measurement and their related purposes.[2]

The more objectives are written in Interval or Ratio scale terms, the more likely the planning, design, development, and implementation will be successful. Fuzzy objectives will not serve us well to guide us in getting from where we are to success.

Means and Ends

Differentiating between means and ends. Almost all performance improvement experts agree on the importance of writing and using measurable performance objectives. Objectives correctly focus on ends and not methods, means, or resources.[3] Ends—"Whats"—sensibly should be identified and defined before we select "How" to get from where we are to our destinations. If we don't select our solutions, methods, resources, and interventions on the basis of what results we are to achieve, what do we have in mind for their selection?

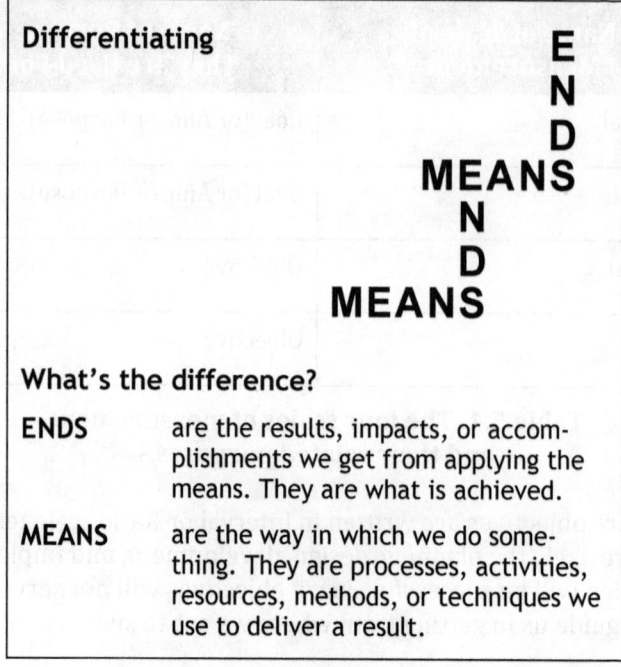

Figure 5.2. The difference between ends and means.

As Figure 5.2 shows, ends and means are different but related. Means are useless if they don't deliver worthwhile ends.

Successful planning focuses first on ends, or results, in measurable terms. This is central for setting objectives, measuring progress, and providing continual improvement toward the important results. Measurable results are vital for determining what to keep, what to fix, and what to abandon (see Table 5.2.).

Objectives and Performance Specifications

Organizational Element	Planning and Focus	Brief Description
Outcomes	Mega	Results and their consequences for external clients and society
Outputs	Macro	The results an organization can or does deliver outside of itself
Products	Micro	The building-block results that are produced within the organization
Processes	Process	The ways, means, activities, procedures, and methods used internally
Inputs	Input	The human, physical, and financial resources that an organization can or does use

Table 5.2. The Organizational Elements, the results related to each, and their definitions.

Objectives state in Interval or Ratio scale terms where you are headed and how to tell when you have arrived. Every objective should meet the following six points:

1. The objective states only ends and never includes means, methods, activities, or how-to-do-its. Ends are "results, achievements, consequences, payoffs, and/or impacts."
2. The objective is measurable on an Interval or Ratio scale.
3. The objective includes four components that aid measurement:
   a. what result is to be accomplished
   b. who or what will demonstrate the accomplished result
   c. under what conditions will the result be observed and measured
   d. what the measurable result will be, in Interval or Ratio scale terms

4. The objective does not include words ending in "ing." Words ending in "ing" are usually a means (e.g., "training," "providing," "producing") and thus should not appear in any useful objective.

5. Useful objectives are based on meeting documented needs—gaps between current results and required results. Useful objectives are based on data rather than perceived wants.

6. Each objective is linked to results and consequences for individuals and small groups, objectives for the organization, and objectives for external clients and society.

Some Examples of Objectives at the Mega, Macro, and Micro Levels[4]

Below is a Mega-level objective (using a military example):

> By the conclusion of Ramadan of next year, non-combatant civilians residing in the Province will suffer no greater rates of violent death or injury than those seen from baseline crime rates in surrounding countries deemed by the United Nations to be "at peace." All coalition force operations will be conducted in accordance with U.S. and international law, as indicated by no upheld successful prosecutions of coalition personnel in military or international courts for offenses causing loss of life, limb, and/or livelihood. There will be no loss of non-combatant civilian life attributed to coalition force operations as certified by Provincial government or United Nations monitors.

Objectives and Performance Specifications

Examples of **Mega**-level objectives, or Outcomes, to be measured include such contributing indicators as health and well-being, consequences of pollution, accidents, discrimination, poverty, substance abuse, disease, shelter, war and/or riot, harm to environment, starvation (or malnutrition), child abuse, partner/spousal abuse, and self-sufficiency. Every organization contributes to the increase or decrease of one or more of these Outcomes, and Mega-level objectives articulate precisely what you choose for that contribution to be.

The second level of objectives, **Macro** objectives, will appear as the Outputs of your organization. Outputs are what an organization can or does deliver outside itself (e.g., manufactured automobiles, competent graduates, defeated adversaries)—not to be confused with the *actual effects* created by delivery of those things in our society, communities, or external clients. A well-defined Output is an unambiguous definition of what your organization delivers into the surrounding marketplace or environment. For example, an output can be the intention to "provide timely aid to victims of natural disaster":

> **After October of this year, at least 99% of all families rendered homeless by any natural disaster will receive adequate emergency shelter within 48 hours after the disaster event ends, where inadequacy is indicated by number of substantiated complaints (including health and nutrition-related consequences) that shelter did not protect occupants from the elements and was unsafe when provided.**

The third level of objectives is **Micro.** These cascade from Mega and Macro objectives. A well-developed objective at the Micro level might state the following corporate example:

> Cellular telephones and bundled accessories delivered to final assembly and to the shipping department will meet all quality acceptance standards and criteria, as indicated by sign-off of the quality inspector on each shift and no greater than 0.2% rejects as reported by the quality assurance test laboratory.

Such a clearly defined objective at the Micro level articulates precisely what the performance target is and how you'll know when you have achieved it. It does not presuppose or include the means, methods, approaches and activities to achieve the objective; instead, it clearly focuses on ends and not means. The usefulness of the Micro-level objectives will be demonstrated contributions to organization as a whole is meeting its purposes (Macro level) or adding value for its external clients and society (Mega level).

The more well-defined your organization's objectives are at the Mega, Macro, and Micro levels, the more your activities will yield success. Vague and foggy won't work well. This is true no matter your context, be it in the public or private sector, for-profit or not-for-profit. Gearing your organization's tasks, Products, Outputs and Outcomes toward useful, productive societal value added requires close attention to alignment of objectives across levels, and to how quality objectives are constructed in the first place.

Traditional planning usually originates at Macro-level—often mislabeled "strategic"—planning. While this is an important part of the process, effective planning must begin at the Mega level.

Ends and Means: Related but Different

Objectives (as well as needs, and needs assessment that are fully discussed in Chapter 7) rely on statements of results, not means (or resources, or activities). The following exercise will let you practice differentiating between ends (results, consequences) and means (how-to's, methods, activities, processes):

Objectives and Performance Specifications

For each item on the list below, put a check in the appropriate column, depending on whether it is primarily an End (results, consequence, or payoff) or a Means (resources, methods, how-to-do-it, intervention, processes, activity, or method):

	End	Means
Learning computer software trouble shooting		
Looking for a job		
Have positive self-esteem		
Training		
Downsizing		
Strategic planning		
Tactical planning		
Operational planning		
Best practices		
College graduate		
Survival		
Negotiating an end to terrorism		
Six Sigma		
Assessing needs		
Benchmarking		
Continual improvement		
Team building		
Loving		

Means vs. Ends Answer Key

	End	Means
Learning computer software trouble shooting		✓
Looking for a job		✓
Have positive self-esteem	✓	
Training		✓
Downsizing		✓
Strategic planning		✓
Tactical planning		✓
Operational planning		✓
Best practices		✓
College graduate	✓	
Survival	✓	
Negotiating an end to terrorism		✓
Six Sigma		✓
Assessing needs		✓
Benchmarking		✓
Continual improvement		✓
Team building		✓
Loving		✓

Just because something is important doesn't mean that it is an end. Negotiating an end to terrorism is a means we all want to be successful but the means of negotiating is not the same as getting the terrorism to end. Similarly, training can be a means to get useful competence and successful performance—an end that is useful. We should not confuse any "how" (a means) with the results, or ends. One verbal cue that you might be dealing with a means is that just about all words in the English language ending with "ing" (planning, developing, evaluating, learning, training, managing, creating) are means. To find out what ends might be related, simply ask, "If we were successful with this means, what would the result be?"

Objectives and Performance Specifications

There is no such thing as something that is not measurable. Objectives at all levels of planning, activity, and results are vital for valid planning. Everything is measurable—measurable on a mathematical scale of measurement (Table 5.1)—so don't deceive yourself into thinking you can dismiss important results as being "intangible" or "not measurable." Doing so denies you the ability to measure your success, failure, or progress toward useful results.

Just saying something is "not measurable" is in itself a measurement: you have distinguished two categories. It is only sensible and rationale to make a commitment to measurable purposes and destinations. Increasingly, organizations throughout the world are increasingly focusing on Mega-level results.[5]

Goals and objectives are related yet different. There are differences between goals and objectives, and regardless of the level—Mega, Macro, Micro—they all should be rigorous and measurable, as shown in Figure 5.3.

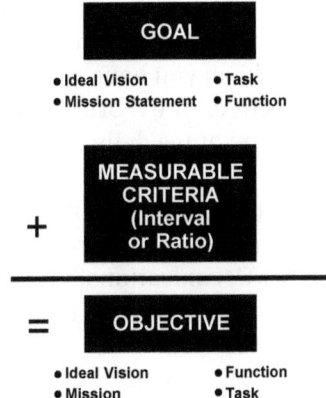

Figure 5.3. The relationship between goals and objectives and their characteristics.[6]

For example, a goal might be "improve the profits of our organization." Adding Interval or Ratio scale criteria would add the criteria to change it to an objective of "increase profits by at least 10% a year for five consecutive years." The goal notes "where we are headed," and the objective precisely adds "how we know when we have arrived."

So no matter whether you are preparing objectives for the societal/Mega level, for the organizational/Macro level, or for the individual performance/Micro level, you should be precise and rigorous: state measurably where you are headed and how you can tell when you have arrived.

A *goal* (or aim or purpose) states where we are headed but does not have rigorous criteria for measuring the accomplishment. An *objective* states both where you are headed and how to precisely tell when you have arrived. The more we state our purposes as objectives, the more confidence we can have of assuring completion of what we deliver.

Ensuring that you have the required characteristics of an objective. To check on your relating ends, means, measurability levels, and the Organizational Elements, Figure 5.4 shows a way to see where you are relative to all of this as shown in an activities progression.

We have been moving along in defining where we should head, based on the Ideal Vision, and the importance of measurable rigor. Now, let's turn our attention to some guides and tools to use as we think and apply Mega.

Objectives and Performance Specifications

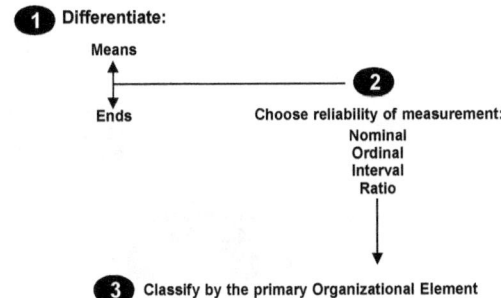

Mega-level ◄──► Macro-level ◄──► Micro-level ◄──► Processes ◄──► Inputs

Figure 5.4. The relationship among ends and means, reliability of measurement, and Organizational Element focus.

Outside-In vs. Inside-Out Planning

Outside-in vs. inside-out planning offers a guide for choosing and delivering societal, community/external client-focused results that you and/or your organization would like to achieve.

Outside-in planning. Beginning with a result (or objective), and track the flow through the Organizational Elements starting from outside/Mega through the other organizational elements, Figure 5.5 Starting from the outside (Mega) and deriving down through the organizational elements will better ensure that the planning will be valid and not assume any linkages.

Inside-out planning. If you are required to be working with others on an existing organizational program or context who want to start from the more "comfortable" and conventional inside-out/upward flow, you must remember if you start inside, make sure that you "roll up" through Macro to Mega and ensure all the external and internal linkages.

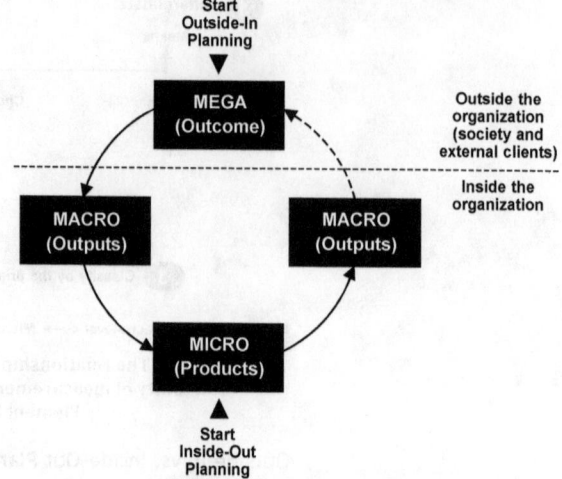

Figure 5.5. Inside-out and outside-in planning cycle.[7]

"Inside-out" is the approach usually done by conventional planners. It is not very often when using this upward flow that people get to precise requirements for Macro or Mega results and consequences, so they miss the assurance that what they use, do, produce, and deliver will add value to all internal and external stakeholders. When starting "inside" their organization or their operational assignments, most people quickly get stuck in their comfort zones and never make the full alignment.[8] If you must start inside the organization, double check the completeness of your analysis by checking to see if it is compatible with the outside-in assessment.

Figure 5.6 shows an algorithm, or job aid, for preparing useful objectives.

Useful Objectives

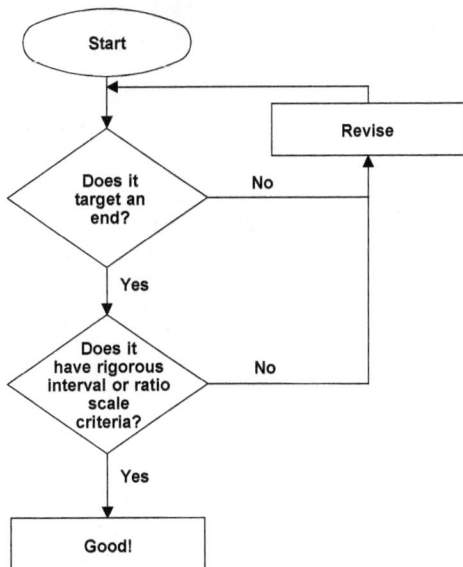

Figure 5.6. A job aid for preparing useful objectives.

It is basic to Mega Thinking and Planning that everything is results focused; everything is precise, rigorous, and measurable.

Action Steps

1. Be very clear, precise, and rigorous concerning where you are headed and how to measure when you have arrived: measurable objectives and their performance specifications.

2. Act on the basis that everything is measurable—measurable on one of four scales of measurement: Nominal, Ordinal, Interval, and Ratio. Don't let anyone get away with thinking and acting that there are just some things that are measurable. Show them.

3. Distinguish between *ends*—results, consequences, performance—and *means*—the ways to deliver results.

4. Act on the basis that there are three levels of planning (Mega, Macro, and Micro) and three levels of associated results (Outcomes, Outputs, and Products). Don't blur these—the differences are operationally critical.

5. Prepare objectives for the three levels of planning. Each objective should state where you are headed and how to tell when you have arrived. Figure 5.5 provides guidance. Objectives never include methods, means, activities, approaches, or resources. Never.

6. Be precise. An objective has Interval or Ratio scale indicators. A goal has only Nominal or Ordinal Scale indicators. Use objectives whenever possible.

7. Planning best starts at the level of society (Mega) and then rolls down inside the organization to Macro and Micro levels.

Objectives and Performance Specifications

Endnotes

1. Not only should everything be measurable, but all should be based on valid research. Some good guidance is provided by the International Society for Performance Improvement (ISPI) principles that include: Focus on results, take a system approach, add value, partner with others, use needs assessment, conduct performance analysis, design to specifications, systematic selection design and development, implement systematically, and evaluate and do continual improvement (ISPI.org).

2. Stevens, S. S. (1951). Mathematics, measurement, and psychophysics. In Stevens, S. S. *Handbook of experimental psychology.* New York: John Wiley & Sons.

   Kaufman, R. A. (1972). *Educational system planning.* Englewood Cliffs, NJ: Prentice-Hall. (Also Planificacion de systemas educativos [translation of *Educational System Planning*]. Mexico City: Editorial Trillas, S.A., 1973).

3. Bob Mager set the original standard for measurable objectives. Later, Tom Gilbert made the important distinction between behavior and performance (between actions and consequences). Recently, some "Constructivists" have had objections to writing objectives because they claim it can cut down on creativity and imposes the planner's values on the clients. This view, I believe, is not useful. For a detailed discussion on the topic of Constructivism, please see the analysis of philosophy professor David Gruender; Gruender, C. D. (May–June, 1996). "Constructivism and learning: A philosophical appraisal. *Educational Technology, 36*(3), 21–29.

   A useful aid is the "Hey Mommy Test." It encourages you to take whatever purpose statement you have prepared (objective) and state, "Hey Mommy, let me show you how I can..." If it is a useful objective, it will provide a reasonable set of criteria.

4. Based on examples in Moore, S., Ellsworth, J. B., & Kaufman, R. (Aug., 2008). Objectives—are they useful? A quick assessment. *Performance Improvement,* (47), 7, pp. 41–47.
5. Kaufman, R., Watkins, R., Triner, D., & Stith, M. (1998). The changing corporate mind: Organizations, visions, mission, purposes, and indicators on the move toward societal payoffs. *Performance Improvement Quarterly,* (11), 3, pp. 32–44.
6. Based on Kaufman, R. (2006). *Change, Choices, and Consequences: A Guide to Mega Thinking and Planning.* Amherst, MA: HRD Press.

   Kaufman, R. (2000). *Mega Planning: Practical tools for organizational success.* Thousand Oaks, CA: Sage Publications. Also *Planificación Mega: Herramientas practices paral el exito organizacional.* (2004). Traducción de Sonia Agut. Universitat Jaume I. Castelló de la Plana, Espana.
7. Kaufman, R. (2000). *Mega Planning: Practical tools for organizational success.* Thousand Oaks, CA: Sage Publications. Also *Planificación Mega: Herramientas practices paral el exito organizacional.* (2004). Traducción de Sonia Agut. Universitat Jaume I. Castelló de la Plana, Espana.
8. Hinchliffe, D. R. (1995). *Training for Results: Determining Education and Training Needs for Emergency Management in Australia.* Unpublished doctoral dissertation. Monash University, Clayton Campus, Victoria, Australia.

Chapter 6

Mission Objectives: Preparing the Objective for Your Organization

A *mission objective* states where an organization is headed and how to tell when it has arrived. Like any other objective (Chapter 5), it states the organizational purpose in clear, precise, and rigorous terms: measurable on an Interval or Ratio scale.

The Mission Objective and Its Relation to Mega

When doing Mega planning, one's organization states, in measurable performance terms, where they are headed and how to tell when they have arrived. This is called a *mission objective*. The mission objective states, again in measurable terms, what elements of the Ideal Vision/Mega the organization commits to deliver. Thus, the Ideal Vision is the basis for the mission objective.

A mission objective states, in measurable performance terms, what results the organization delivers as it moves ever closer to meeting the Mega level needs selected for closure. Figure 6.1 provides the "roll down" relationships between Mega, Macro, and Micro results, and this relationship is useful so that you always relate the levels of contributions for each level of results.

The mission objective states clearly what the organization (and all of its internal partners) will deliver and never includes the methods or resources to be used. It is like any other objective.

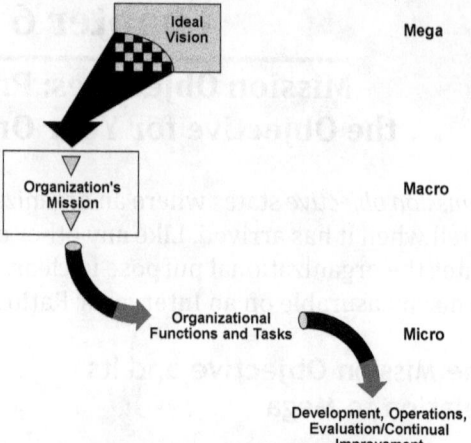

Missions derive from the Ideal Vision. An organization selects what portion of the Ideal Vision it commits to deliver and move ever closer to it.

Figure 6.1. The alignment and "rolldown" relationship among Mega/Ideal Vision, Macro (mission objective), and Micro (individual performance contributions).[1]

Mission Objective

Based on the Mega level needs—gaps in results (covered in Chapter 7 on needs assessment)—to be closed, the mission objective can be derived by the planning team. Here is a simulated mission objective:

> *Any production and delivered food outputs of this factory will result in zero loss of life for all clients, disabilities, and losses of income for individuals, families, or others consuming what is delivered. In addition, there will be no disabling injuries, illnesses, or death from any organizational associate related to the manufacturing and delivery of our food.*

Mission Objectives

A mission objective states, in measurable performance terms, what results the organization delivers as it moves ever closer to meeting the Mega level needs selected for closure. Figure 6.1 provides the "roll down" relationships between Mega, Macro, and Micro results, and this relationship is useful so that you always relate the levels of contributions for each level of results.

Sometimes, there is a mission objective already derived for your organization. Figure 6.2 presents an exercise to determine if a mission objective is useful.

MISSIONS: Are they appropriate? A Procedure

	Target		Results/Ends Level		
Mission Elements:	Ends	Means	Mega	Macro	Micro
a)					
b)					
c)					

Steps:
1) List each element of the mission.
2) For each element, determine if it relates to an End or a Means.
3) If an element relates to an End, determine if it is focused at the Mega, Macro, or Micro level.
4) If an element is related to a Means, or to a Macro or Micro result, ask, "**What results and payoffs would I get if I got or accomplished this?**" Keep asking the same question until an End is identified. If you continue this question, you will ultimately get to Mega.

Figure 6.2. A procedure for ensuring that your mission objective is correctly stated.

Try putting your (or any) mission objective through this "filter." It can provide some additional comfort to you to ensure that what you are using will contribute to success, or it will tell you what is missing to that you can make it useful and complete.

The Manager's Pocket Guide to Mega Thinking and Planning

To ensure that your objectives, all objectives, link all three levels of results and consequences, see the job aid in Figure 6.3.

Ensuring an Objective Links to All 3 Levels of Results

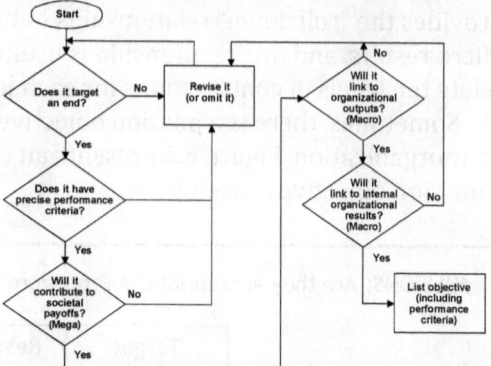

Ensuring that your objective is useful at all three levels of planning and results.

Figure 6.3. A job aid for ensuring that your objectives link all three levels of results.

An example of including Mega in objectives and performance criteria. The city commissioners and city manager of Tallahassee, Florida, wanted to be able to prove to citizens that their tax money was being used wisely. Using Mega thinking and planning, they reviewed their existing performance objectives and added Mega criteria to some.[2] For example, they added the consequences of first responders showing up (damage avoided or reduced and crime stopped are impact reduced) to their criteria, not just the time that it took them to respond. Not only were services delivered, but also the city sought indicators of the value added by the first responders once they arrived.

Mission Objectives

The next step in applying a mission objective when doing Mega planning is to identify gaps between current ability to meet these mission-level requirements and the required performance (including critical elements such as ingredients, processing methods, handling, shipping, and delivery). This is needs assessment and is defined and provided next in Chapter 7.

From these gaps, alternative methods and means could be identified, such as use of remote scanning, sniffers, visual inspections, and safety checks at all levels of production and delivery. Next, the building-block functions, or individual products (Micro level), can be derived to define and deliver the results that have to be accomplished to get from What Is to What Should Be.[3]

Action Steps

1. Prepare objectives—the mission objective—for your organization that, like any other objectives, state Interval or Ratio Scale terms where you are headed and how to tell when you have arrived.

2. The mission objective is derived from the Ideal Vision and states which elements of the Ideal Vision the organization commits to move closer toward and deliver. This decision will be based on a needs assessment, covered in Chapter 7.

3. Every objective you derive for your success must add value to all three levels of results: Mega, Macro, and Micro. Figure 6.3 will be helpful.

Endnotes

1. Kaufman, R. (2006). *Change, Choices, and Consequences: A Guide to Mega Thinking and Planning.* Amherst, MA: HRD Press, Inc.

2. City of Tallahassee Auditor, May 20, 2009. Community and Organizational Vital Signs, Tallahassee, Florida.

3. The methods and concepts for developing mission profiles and detailed system analyses are provided in Kaufman, R. (1998). *Strategic thinking: A guide to identifying and solving problems. Revised.* Washington, D.C., and Arlington, VA: The International Society for Performance Improvement and the American Society for Training and Development.

Chapter 7

Needs and Needs Assessment

Perhaps the most over-worked word in the English language is "need." It is usually confused with "want" or "really, really want."

In planning, as we have noted earlier, the distinction between ends and means is critical; first define and justify where you want to be, and then select the means to get there. Vital to Mega Thinking and Planning is defining "need" as a gap in results, not a gap in means or resources. It really is important, although the distinction might seem trivial at first.

Need is NOT a Verb![1]

Conventional English-language usage would have us employ the common word "need" as a verb (or in a verb sense)—to identify means, methods, activities, and actions and/or resources we desire or intend to use. Terms such as "need to," "need for," "needing," and "needed" are common, conventional, and destructive to useful planning. This is important because we have already seen that it is important to distinguish means from ends. When you use "need" as a verb, you are jumping into a solution—actually demanding a solution such as "we need more money"—before defining what gaps in results and selecting a means that will close that performance gap.

As hard as it is to change our own behavior (and most of us who want others to change seem to resist it the most ourselves!), it is central to useful planning to distinguish between ends and means. We have noted this in Chapter 4 as Critical Success Factor 2. To do reasonable and justifiable planning, we have to (1) focus on ends and not means and, thus, (2) use "need" as a noun. Need, for useful and successful planning, is only used as a noun—as a gap between current and desired results as shown in Figure 7.1.

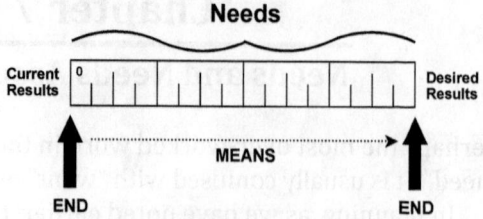

Figure 7.1. A need (as a noun) is a gap between current results and required results.[2]

If we use "need" as a noun, we will be able to both justify useful objectives as well as be able to justify what we do and deliver—evaluation based on comparing our objectives with our results—on the basis of costs-consequences analysis. We will be able to defend everything we use, do, produce, and deliver. It is the only sensible way we can demonstrate value added.[3]

Needs, Nouns, Verbs, and Conflict

Many arguments, conflicts, and misunderstandings are because common language uses "need" as a verb, such as "we need more time," "we need more money," "we need to economize," "we need to outsource," "we need to reorganize." Thus, people unthinking or unknowingly jump into solutions before defining and justifying a problem. (A *problem* is a need chosen for reduction or elimination.)

By jumping into a solution—a means, methods, intervention, technique, or tool—by using "need" as a verb, the arguments can begin! We can argue almost endlessly about which means is better if we don't define what gap in results a means will close. To reduce conflict as well as select solutions-in-search-of-problems, simply go back to basics: first define the needs (as gaps in results) and then consider and select the means to close those gaps in results. "Need" is an over-used word. And the way it is conventionally used leads on to means before defining and justifying the ends to be accomplished. People confuse needs and wants (ends and means) all the time. And the consequences of getting these confused are not pretty. Ever hear a family member say things like:

- *I need new shoes.*
- *I need a new car.*
- *I need a new dress/suit.*
- *I need to go to the mall.*
- *I need more allowance.*
- *I need more money.*
- *I need...*

Well, you get the idea. They use "need" as a verb so that it takes away your (and their) choices. When one uses "need" as a verb, it is very demanding: no options, no choices...just the solution (more money, new car) that they have pre-selected. Thus, people are constantly picking solutions before they know the problems.

Needs Are Not Wants, and Means Are Not Ends

Understand, please, that everything that is called a "need" or a "needs assessment" really might not be real needs nor needs assessments. Following is an exercise that could help you and your partners sort out what are needs and needs assessments.

Foggy World-Wide Industries: A hypothetical case study.[4]
Here is a hypothetical example of the results of a "needs assessment" done by Foggy World-Wide Industries:

The Manager's Pocket Guide to Mega Thinking and Planning

> **Foggy World-Wide Industries**
> **"Needs Assessment" Summary**
> 1. "We have to have everyone be managing with vision."
> 2. "We need to be world class."
> 3. "We have to be competitive."
> 4. "We need more executive development and training."
> 5. "We need to cut production cycle time."
> 6. "A need exists to make quality our first priority."
> 7. "We must all work together as partners."
> 8. "We must increase our production by 18%."
> 9. "There must be no deaths or disabling injuries from what we deliver."
> 10. "We must make a net-net-net profit each and every year."
> 11. "We must not bring harm to living things."
> 12. "We need to use performance technology."

Examine each of the above "needs assessment" statements and identify which elements of each are.

- a **need** as a gap in results; or
- a **quasi-need:** a "need" as a gap in methods or a gap in resources.

And for each need identified, classify it as

- **Mega**/outcome related;
- **Macro**/output related; or
- **Micro**/product related.

Needs and Needs Assessment

Let's compare answers:

1. *We have to have everyone managing with vision.*

    The word "managing" is the key here. It is a means (Process). It states nothing about what results and payoffs there will be from "managing with vision" nor does it state what the vision will be.

2. *We "need" to be world class.*

    This aspiration never defines what "world class" is or how we would measure it. It also does not state what the results and payoffs will be from being "world class." If we don't know current results, we cannot determine if there are gaps between that and whatever "world class" means. This does not relate to a need but is an intention, and a blurry one at that.

3. *We have to be competitive.*

    This aspiration never defines what "competitive" is or how we would measure it. It also does not state what the results and payoffs will be from being "competitive." This does not relate to a need but is an intention, and—like #2—another hazy one.

4. *We "need" more executive development and training.*

    This is a means. Your first clue that it is, is the use of "need" as a verb, which makes it a means—executive development and training—without defining the ends to be accomplished. In this case, what gap in results would be closed by "more executive development and training"? What gap in results would this deliver at the Mega, Macro, and Micro levels?

5. *We "need" to cut production cycle time.*

    This is also a means. Your clue again is the use of "need" as a verb, which makes it a means—reducing production cycle time—without defining the ends to be accomplished. In this case, what gap in results would be closed by "cutting down on production cycle time"? What gap in results would this deliver at the Mega, Macro, and Micro levels?

6. *A "need" exists to make quality our first priority.*

   Again, this is a means. Your clue is the use of "need" in a verb sense—limiting means without defining the ends to be accomplished. In this case, what gap in results would be closed by "making quality our first priority"? What *is* "quality" and how do we measure it? What gap in results would this deliver at the Mega, Macro, and Micro levels.

7. *We must all work together as partners.*

   This is also a means; work together is a process. In this case, what gap in results would be closed by "working together as partners"? What gap in results would "working together" deliver at the Mega, Macro, and Micro levels?

8. *We must increase our production by 18%.*

   At least, a result...at the Micro level. If it were stated as a "need"—a gap between current results and desired ones—it might be stated: "current production of at least 18%." It is interesting that this one doesn't also specify that there will be no increase in rejections; one could increase production by the amount requested while making rejections, and re-works increase by 125%.

9. *There must be no deaths or disabling injuries from what we deliver.*

   This will deliver results at the Mega level. If stated as a need, it might read "Last year there were three disabling injuries and one death from our Outputs. Next year and following there will be no disabling injuries and no deaths from our Outputs."

10. *We must make a net-net-net profit each and every year.*

    This will deliver results at the Mega level...to the extent to which profit is earned without bringing harm to anyone or the environment. Profit over time is an indicator of a Mega-level contribution. If stated as a need, it might read "Last year we had a loss of $2.23 million. Next year—and following—we will increase our profits by at least 5% every year."

Needs and Needs Assessment

This one is a bit tricky: profit alone would be Macro but since it is continual each and every year, it is an indicator of doing no harm to external clients and society. If harm were done (death, toxic disabling pollution, fraud, etc.), the profits would likely be reduced or even thrown into an operating loss.

11. *We must not bring harm to living things.*

    This will deliver results at the Mega level to the extent that what our organization does and delivers does not bring harm to the environment and living things. We are "good neighbors." If stated as a need, it might read, "Last year we had two spills cited by the environmental council for being toxic and destructive; next year and each and every year following we will have no incidents causing toxic damage or other kinds of destruction."

12. *We "need" to use performance technology.*

    "Performance technology" is a means, even though it could be a very powerful means if used at the right time with the right people under the correct conditions. Ask, "If we were successful at using performance technology, what would the results of that be?"

    Also, notice that *none* of **Foggy World-Wide Industries'** "needs" were stated as gaps in results. This is a common mistake, and one you can avoid. Also, notice how many times "need" was used as a verb ("we 'need' to use performance technology") and thus moving anything the organization uses, does, and delivers toward a focus on solutions rather than results and value added.

So making sure that you use "need" as a noun—as a gap in results—is vital to define where you are headed and justify why you want to get there.

> **Definitions**
>
> - A *need* is a gap between current results and desired or required results; a noun.
>
> - A *needs assessment* identifies the gaps between current and desired results (best including needs at the Mega, Macro, and Micro levels) and places them in priority order on the basis of the costs to meet the needs as compared to the costs to ignore the needs.
>
> - A *problem* is a *need* selected for elimination or reduction.

Working with Needs as Gaps in Results

Choosing the right level for a needs assessment is vital. The best starting place is at Mega because everything your organization uses, does, produces, and delivers must add value to society. Figure 7.2 provides a guide for doing a needs assessment. It includes the following:

1.0 Decide to plan using needs (gaps in results) not wants (preferred solutions).

2.0 Identify planning partners, including representative implementers, recipients of what your work will deliver, and society.

3.0 Select the representatives for needs assessment and planning.

4.0 Obtain the planning partners' commitment, including to do Mega Thinking and Planning.

5.0 Select the needs assessment planning framework: Mega, Macro, or Micro. Again, if you don't start at Mega, you are either certain that you will add value to society or you are willing to risk that you will.

Needs and Needs Assessment

6.0 Collect the "hard" performance data on gaps in results.

7.0 At the same time as collecting "hard" data, collect "soft" data—perceptions of gaps in results.

8.0 Determine the matches and mismatches (agreements and disagreements) between the "hard" and "soft" data and reconcile any differences, including collecting more data.

9.0 Prioritize the needs based on the costs to meet the needs as compared to the costs to ignore the needs.

10.0 Select the needs to be eliminated or reduced.

11.0 Obtain approvals and revise as required.

To help you in needs assessment, Figures 7.2 and 7.3 provide some guides.

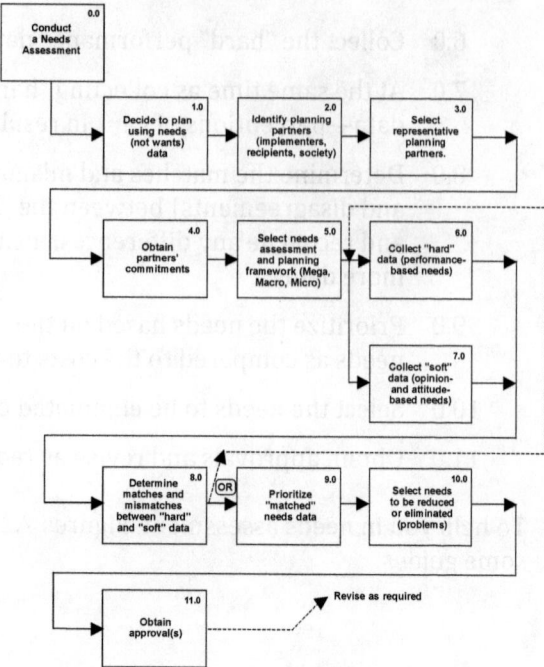

Figure 7.2. The functions to be completed to do a needs assessment.[5]

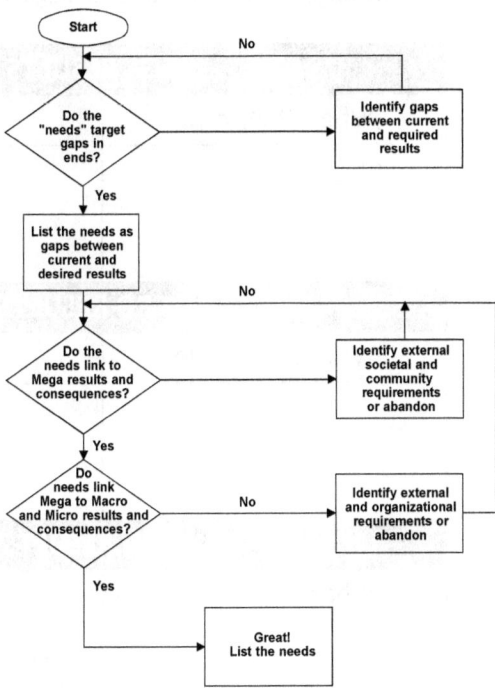

Figure 7.3. Ensuring that your needs assessment attends to needs as gaps in results and links to all three levels of planning: Mega, Macro, and Micro.[6]

Recording Your Needs Assessment Data

Based on the discussion of the Organizational Elements Model (OEM), in order to identify needs at each level, please complete Table 7.1 with examples that apply to your personal and/or professional life (your choice of which one).

MEGA RESULTS	
What Should Be	What Is

MACRO RESULTS	
What Should Be	What Is

MICRO RESULTS	
What Should Be	What Is

PROCESSES	
What Should Be	What Is

INPUTS	
What Should Be	What Is

Table 7.1. A table for recording needs (gaps in results) for each of the Organizational Elements.

Needs and Needs Assessment

Not everything called a "needs assessment" is really useful, and some are possibly harmful. Just about anything gets called a "need assessment." Most of the time, it is really a "wants assessment" because it is processes and solutions that are desired. As an example of the confusion, a popular method in the literature (and indeed popular in practice as well) is a "training needs assessment." If you believe the writings of Deming[7] and Juran[8] and if you do *training needs assessment,* you will be wrong 80 or 90 percent of the time.

Why? Each of these noted professionals note that 80 or 90 percent of all breakdowns are not individual performance (Micro/Products) breakdowns but system (Macro or Mega) breakdowns. So if you only fix something—no matter how well or how cleverly—at the individual performance level (through such interventions as training, performance technology, job aids, electronic performance supports), then you will only be right a very small percentage of the time. You can spend a lot of time, effort, and money at the Micro/Product level and if the breakdowns are above, then you have wasted many resources and probably frustrated the people involved.

Three bonuses for using "need" as a noun. There is a 3-for-1 sale for using "need" as the gap in results between current results and consequences and desired results and consequences:

1. The What Should Be criteria serve as your measurable objectives—your performance criteria—for specifying where you are headed and how to tell when you have arrived. Successful performance design and development requires that we state our objectives in measurable performance terms, ideally on an Interval or Ratio Scale. Defining "need" in this way yields such objectives, and they are based on actual performance.

2. The gaps between current results (What Is) and desired/required results (What Should Be) provide the basis for sensible, sensitive, and justifiable evaluation. That is a positive bonus, for that comes with using "need" as a noun.

Usually we get told "we don't have the time and or resources for evaluation," and this answers that invalid objection to doing evaluations. (Interesting how some people don't have the time or resources to do an evaluation but have to come up with them when an intervention or program fails.)

By using "need" as a gap in results, one only has to plot the extent to which performance results have migrated from the previous What Is for results to the What Should Be for results. The extent to which the gap in results has been reduced or eliminated is the evaluation—evaluation based on performance data.

3. Using need as a noun allows you to justify where you are headed, why you want to get there, and what are the payoffs for doing so. It provides an almost bullet-proof rationale for any proposed work or activities. Let's see.

Getting an edge when writing proposals. Most proposals get turned down because they "cost too much," "there is not enough time," or "there are not enough resources." This negative decision may be made if one only proposed based on the cost to meet the needs—the costs to close the gaps in results.

Now, based on the third bonus for defining "need" as a noun, when you collect solid data on the gaps (best at the Mega, Macro, and Micro levels), you may price out (a) the costs to meet the needs and (b) the costs to ignore the needs. This is a major difference with conventional approaches to proposing programs, projects, or activities.

If you provide the decision maker with both the costs to meet the needs as well as the costs to ignore the needs (think about the costs for not having safe oil tankers, for not having non-roll-over cars, for not having safe food or medicines), the decision maker becomes accountable for not meeting the needs if he or she decides not to go ahead with meeting the needs you have specified based on valid data.

When estimates of *costs-consequences* based on Mega and needs assessment as defined here have been accomplished, there is a solid base for making decisions.[9] Applications have varied

Needs and Needs Assessment

from industry to state government, including the Florida Division of Blind Services, Refinor (Argentina), State of Ohio Workforce Development, Sonora Institute of Technology, to name a few.[10]

Needs at the Mega level—an incomplete example. Using the example of Hurricane Katrina in New Orleans (with hypothetical numbers), let's explore needs as gaps in results. Here is a partial table to show needs as gaps in results:

What Is	What Should/Could Be
X people dead, Y people suffer disabling injury	0 dead or injured
$X billion plus property damage from storms	0 property damage from storms
X displaced people with no jobs or sources of income	0 displaced people All residents self-sufficient and self-reliant
X miles of polluted city with severe health hazard potential	0 pollution 0 health hazard from pollution
Income loss to government of $Y	0 loss of government income from natural causes (e.g., storms)
Z looters arrested and in jail from citizen, public, and business loss of property	0 criminality 0 losses from illegal activity
Flood damage to levees making them dangerous for future storms	No vulnerability from levee failures from future storms or flooding
Medical supplies and medical treatment not available for immunization and decontamination resulting in permanent and disablement of residents	No reduction of self-sufficiency and self-reliance based on lack of response, medical supplies, and treatment
Etc.	

For each element at the Mega level, there are gaps in results identified. These all are related to Mega results and consequences. Not practical or real world? Just put yourself in the shoes of those impacted by storms and see if these gaps in results should not be closed. Can we achieve closure for all? We ethically have to see how close we can get in the future.

To ensure that you link all three levels of planning and results in your Mega Thinking and Planning, use the job aid in Figure 7.3.

Needs, Needs Assessment, and Evaluation: Related Yet Different

This concept is so vital to successful planning and performance improvement, it is covered in Chapter 9. Needs assessments are proactive before-the-fact determination of gaps while evaluations identify gaps in results after an intervention, program, or activity.

The basis for useful results and consequences are essential for Mega Thinking and Planning. The basis for planning serves as the criteria for design, development, implementation, evaluation, and continual improvement. It is vital that everything any organization uses, does, produces, and delivers is driven by valid results. And these results are derived from a valid and appropriate needs assessment.

The use of rigorous and useful tools for determining needs and objectives will be vital in dealing with change, choices, and consequence.

Needs assessments are the bases for establishing validating goals and objectives based on performance data. Because they are based on the gaps in results and the costs to meet the needs as compared to the costs to ignore them, a needs assessment allows one to identify and justify any objectives. Rather than relying on judgment, intuition, precedents or authority, needs assessments provide the direction and justification for the following:

Needs and Needs Assessment

1. where you are headed
2. justification, based on data, of why you want to get there
3. how you know when you have arrived (performance criteria for evaluation and continual improvement)

Providing such performance data is not only sensible, but it is safe—a good basis for making good choices and making decisions.

How your organization goes about planning using needs assessment. Following are some considerations for you and your organization to calibrate how you go about planning (and the implications for the basic concepts of Mega Thinking and Planning).[11] For each item, identify your current use of needs assessment and what you should be doing. This form may be used with others in your organization to obtain both insights and agreement.

The Manager's Pocket Guide to Mega Thinking and Planning

WHAT IS					HOW THE ORGANIZATION PERCEIVES NEEDS ASSESSMENT	WHAT SHOULD BE				
1 - Rarely, if ever	2 - Not usually	3 - Sometimes	4 - Frequently	5 - Consistently	Respond to each item below using the following scale. Use this scale for both **What Is** and **What Should Be**. 1 - Rarely, if ever 2 - Not usually 3 - Sometimes 4 - Frequently 5 - Consistently	1 - Rarely, if ever	2 - Not usually	3 - Sometimes	4 - Frequently	5 - Consistently
①	②	③	④	⑤	1. We formally plan.	①	②	③	④	⑤
①	②	③	④	⑤	2. We do needs assessment.	①	②	③	④	⑤
①	②	③	④	⑤	3. Needs assessment is valued in our organization.	①	②	③	④	⑤
①	②	③	④	⑤	4. We use the data from needs assessment to decide what to do.	①	②	③	④	⑤
①	②	③	④	⑤	5. Our needs assessment looks at the gaps between obtained results and predetermined objectives.	①	②	③	④	⑤
①	②	③	④	⑤	6. Needs assessments are results focused.	①	②	③	④	⑤
①	②	③	④	⑤	7. Management is focused on results accomplished (rather than processes and activities engaged in) when it requests a needs assessment.	①	②	③	④	⑤
①	②	③	④	⑤	8. The organization's culture is focused on results.	①	②	③	④	⑤
①	②	③	④	⑤	9. Needs assessment is seen as comparing current results against those results that should be accomplished.	①	②	③	④	⑤
①	②	③	④	⑤	10. Needs assessments are done for strategic planning.	①	②	③	④	⑤
①	②	③	④	⑤	11. Needs assessments are shared with our internal stakeholders.	①	②	③	④	⑤

(continued)

Needs and Needs Assessment

(continued)

1 – Rarely, if ever
2 – Not usually
3 – Sometimes
4 – Frequently
5 - Consistently

WHAT IS	HOW THE ORGANIZATION PERCEIVES NEEDS ASSESSMENT	WHAT SHOULD BE
① ② ③ ④ ⑤	12. Needs assessment results are shared with our external stakeholders.	① ② ③ ④ ⑤
① ② ③ ④ ⑤	13. Needs assessments include a focus on all results to be accomplished by the organization for external clients and society.	① ② ③ ④ ⑤
① ② ③ ④ ⑤	14. Needs assessments include a focus on all of the levels of results—individual performance, small group performance, individual departmental performance, the organization itself—to be accomplished within the organization.	① ② ③ ④ ⑤
① ② ③ ④ ⑤	15. Needs assessments collect actual performance data about units within the organization.	① ② ③ ④ ⑤
① ② ③ ④ ⑤	16. Needs assessments collect actual performance data about the organization itself.	① ② ③ ④ ⑤
① ② ③ ④ ⑤	17. Needs assessments collect actual performance data about the impact on our external clients and society (our neighbors both near and far).	① ② ③ ④ ⑤
① ② ③ ④ ⑤	18. Needs assessments are done to provide useful information for defining *future* directions for the organization.	① ② ③ ④ ⑤

(continued)

(continued)

1 - Rarely, if ever
2 - Not usually
3 - Sometimes
4 - Frequently
5 - Consistently

WHAT IS					HOW THE ORGANIZATION PERCEIVES NEEDS ASSESSMENT	WHAT SHOULD BE				
①	②	③	④	⑤	19. Plans are made on the basis of the desired consequences of results for external clients and society and community (those people who are our close and distant neighbors).	①	②	③	④	⑤
①	②	③	④	⑤	20. Plans are made on the basis of desired individual performance.	①	②	③	④	⑤
①	②	③	④	⑤	21. Plans are made on the basis of results desired for external clients and society and community (those to whom we deliver things or services).	①	②	③	④	⑤
①	②	③	④	⑤	22. Plans are derived from the data obtained from a needs assessment.	①	②	③	④	⑤
①	②	③	④	⑤	23. Data from a needs assessment are used to link resources to activities, programs, projects.	①	②	③	④	⑤
①	②	③	④	⑤	24. Data from a needs assessment are used to link resources to results that add value for external clients.*	①	②	③	④	⑤
①	②	③	④	⑤	25. The organization defines and uses needs assessments for identifying gaps in results for impact on external clients.	①	②	③	④	⑤

(continued)

---

* Sometimes our external clients have clients themselves. Include these links in your response.

Needs and Needs Assessment

(concluded)

1 – Rarely, if ever
2 – Not usually
3 – Sometimes
4 – Frequently
5 - Consistently

WHAT IS	HOW THE ORGANIZATION PERCEIVES NEEDS ASSESSMENT	WHAT SHOULD BE
① ② ③ ④ ⑤	26. The organization defines and uses needs assessments for identifying gaps in results for impact on our society (e.g., health, safety, well-being, survival).	① ② ③ ④ ⑤
① ② ③ ④ ⑤	27. Needs are formally prioritized on the basis of the costs to close gaps in results as compared to the costs of ignoring them.	① ② ③ ④ ⑤
① ② ③ ④ ⑤	28. The organization uses data from a needs assessment to set objectives.	① ② ③ ④ ⑤
① ② ③ ④ ⑤	29. Needs assessment data are used to determine what gaps in results should be addressed.	① ② ③ ④ ⑤
① ② ③ ④ ⑤	30. Needs assessment data are used to prioritize the needs—gaps in results.	① ② ③ ④ ⑤
① ② ③ ④ ⑤	31. Needs assessment data are used to select the best ways and means to meet the needs—gaps in results.	① ② ③ ④ ⑤
① ② ③ ④ ⑤	32. The organization uses needs assessment data as the basis for evaluation.	① ② ③ ④ ⑤
① ② ③ ④ ⑤	33. Needs assessments are seen by associates in the organization as providing important information.	① ② ③ ④ ⑤

These needs assessment-related statements should serve you and your associates as a checklist for doing and using needs assessments as a basis for Mega Thinking and Planning.

Start the dialog about useful planning and use the Six Critical Success Factors (Table 4.1) to guide you. You can get a calibration of "What Is" and "What Should Be" concerning conducting a needs assessment from the responses by yourself and, ideally, other key people associated with your organization.

Needs assessment. It has already been noted that when one does a useful needs assessment

- needs are defined as gaps in results, not gaps in resources (Inputs) or processes/activities/solutions (Processes);
- there are three levels of results—the Mega, Macro, and Micro levels—and thus there are three levels of needs assessment;
- needs are linking among the three levels of planning and results; and
- a *quasi need* is a gap, but not a gap in results; they are gaps in Inputs or Processes.

When identifying needs (as, of course, gaps in results) they are best in Interval or Ratio scale terms (see Table 5.1). The more precise and rigorous you can sensibly be, the better your chances of getting useful results.

Hard and soft data. There are two kinds of data to be collected. Both are important and useful:

    Hard Data: Independently verifiable

    Soft Data: Personal and not independently verifiable

Needs and Needs Assessment

Hard data can be collected in many ways and from many sources. We can go to organizational records and public records. We can get data on sales, returns, production rates and rejects, absences, complaints, etc. There is a lot more data available from public and internal sources than most people at first realize.

Soft data may be collected with questionnaires, inventories, interviews, and meetings.

Doing Needs Assessments

Tips on developing a needs assessment questionnaire. Sometimes it will be useful to develop a needs assessment questionnaire, so following are some guides in checklist format for deriving a useful one:

- ❏ 1. Make certain that the questions are about *results,* not about Processes or Inputs.
- ❏ 2. Ask about perceptions of gaps in *results* for both dimensions—What Is and What Should Be.
- ❏ 3. Ask questions about the three levels of needs:
    - external contributions (Mega)
    - organizational contributions (Macro)
    - building-block internal and operational results (Micro)
- ❏ 4. Have evidence of appropriate validity and reliability of the questions and the sample.
- ❏ 5. Make the questionnaire long enough to get reliable responses, but short enough that people will actually respond.
- ❏ 6. Use an approach that makes it clear to respondents exactly what is wanted. People usually don't want to write long answers, so a checklist or multiple-choice format will reduce their burden while making the questionnaire easier to score.

❑ 7. Don't ask questions that reveal, directly or indirectly, a bias. Don't use the data-collection vehicle to set up the responses you really want.

❑ 8. Ask several questions about each dimension or issue. Ask about each concern in different ways to increase the liability of responses. Basing any decision on answers to one question is risky.

❑ 9. Try out the data-collection instrument on a sample group to identify problems in meaning, coverage, and scorability. Revise it as required. (This step is the same as the sixth step in the problem-solving model, continuous improvement.)

When collecting performance (or "hard" data):

❑ 10. Make certain the data collected relate to important questions for which you want answers.

❑ 11. Assure yourself that the data are collected correctly and that the methods used for gathering it and reporting it are free of any bias.

❑ 12. Assure yourself that the data are based on enough observations to make them reliable, not a one-shot happening.

❑ 13. Make certain that the data can be independently verified and cross-checked.

When the hard data and soft data disagree. Sometimes there will be differences between the "hard" performance data and the "soft" perception data. When this disagreement happens, probe deeper. Both types of data are important because sometimes personal observations find things that the hard data collection did not ask for or collect and this gives you the opportunity to see if there is something substantial to the perceptions. With a dialog with your planning partners, decide which data are more useful.

Having the data from these will be basic to your evaluation where one compares obtained results with intentions.

Applying Needs Assessment Data Collection and Application to an Entire Organization

When a *need* is defined as a gap between current and desired/required results, this allows for some important applications; doing an organizational assessment of needs.

When applying needs assessment to a large organization, the gaps-in-results may be determined for each of the planning/results areas: Mega/Outcomes, Macro/Outputs, and Micro/Products as seen in Figure 7.4.

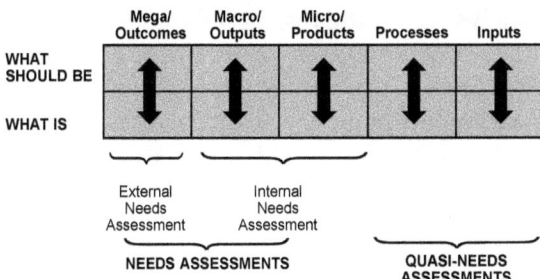

Figure 7.4. The Organizational Elements Model is arrayed on two levels—What Should Be and What Is—and may be used to diagnose organizations.[12]

By collecting needs data for the three levels of results, one can identify the gaps that exist, prioritize each, and then use this to define gaps and areas for organizational improvement. When the gaps exist at the Mega level, then changes could be considered for the Macro, Micro, and then Processes and Inputs levels. This would allow for the alignment and linking that is required for choosing organizational success based on Mega Thinking and Planning.

By using this schema, one might easily see that any gaps in results at below the Mega level must be linked and aligned with the levels above. The nature of the organizational system—starting at Mega—is vital, and this framework helps everyone see the overall context for thinking, planning, doing, delivering, and evaluating.

To use with an organization as a kind of "organizational analysis," use the two-tiered framework in Figure 7.4 and sort the date concerning gaps in results into the proper boxes. When you get the data inserted, you can see what is missing (empty cells or incomplete data) and if the data link from Mega to Macro to Micro to Process to Input. This sounds a bit complex, but it isn't. And you will note where there are disconnects and problems.

Selecting your needs assessment level. Figure 7.5 provides decisions you should make.

It is important that if you start your needs assessment at any other level than Mega you either know that what you use, do, produce, and deliver will add measurable value to society or that you are willing to risk that it will.

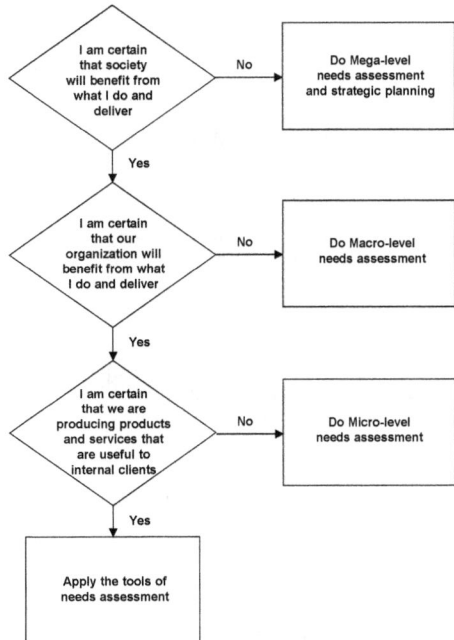

Figure 7.5. A job aid for deciding the level of your needs assessment.[13]

Steps in doing a useful Mega/Ideal Vision level needs assessment. Table 7.2 lists the steps for performing a Mega level needs assessment and a management "score card" for scheduling and tracking progress.

The Manager's Pocket Guide to Mega Thinking and Planning

	Person or Group Responsible	Date Assigned	Date Completed
Determine needs—gaps in results—for each component (or "family of components" in the Ideal Vision).			
Prioritize the needs on the basis of the costs to meet the needs as compared to the costs to ignore them (these might be course-grained estimates).			
Determine your organization's current impact on external clients and society in terms of survival, self-sufficiency, and quality of life.			
Determine the component(s) of the Ideal Vision your organization is committed to deliver and moving ever-closer toward, including indicators of its impact on the survival, self-sufficiency, and quality of life of its external clients and our shared society.			
Place Mega level needs (gaps in results) between the Ideal Vision and the current status, in a priority order, based on the cost to successfully address the problem versus the cost to ignore the problem.			
Develop an Ideal Vision–linked Mission Objective that includes specific criteria for each gap you choose to address (e.g., what you will have accomplished five, ten, or more years from now).			
Break down your Mission Objective to functional building-block objectives.			

(continued)

Needs and Needs Assessment

	Person or Group Responsible	Date Assigned	Date Completed
Obtain formal approval and concurrence of your Macro level needs from your clients as well as your internal partners (clients are included throughout the entire process).			
List alternative methods and means for addressing your Mega level need(s) and identify the advantages and disadvantages of each: costs and consequences.			

Table 7.2. Steps in conducting a Mega level needs assessment.

The same rationale is used for doing a needs assessment for each level of planning and results (see Table 7.3 and Table 7.4). This assessment data will allow you to develop a practical and justifiable mission objective:

	Person or Group Responsible	Date Assigned	Date Completed
Specify the desired quality—useful contributions—of what your organization delivers to external clients. (Remember, starting here assumes—or actually builds on the Mega level needs assessment—that you have linked to the Ideal Vision level.)			
Determine the performance requirements in terms of what your organization delivers, in measurable performance terms, to external clients.			
List the identified and agreed upon need(s).			

(continued)

	Person or Group Responsible	Date Assigned	Date Completed
Align the needs identified at the Macro level with the Ideal Vision and mission of your organization.			
Place Macro level needs in a priority order, based on the cost to ignore versus the cost to meet each identified need.			
Obtain concurrence of the Macro level needs from your internal and external clients.			
List alternative methods and means for addressing your Macro level need(s) and identify the advantages and disadvantages of each.			

Table 7.3. Steps in conducting a Macro level needs assessment.

The same thinking and process holds as you move down to Micro level needs assessment.

	Person or Group Responsible	Date Assigned	Date Completed
Determine individuals' and/or small groups' required performance in measurable terms. (Note that starting at this level assumes linkages to the Macro and Mega levels or you actually have the identified needs from these two levels.)			
Determine individuals' and/or small groups' current performance status relative to the required performance standards established in the first step.			

(continued)

Needs and Needs Assessment

	Person or Group Responsible	Date Assigned	Date Completed
List the identified, agreed upon Micro level need(s).			
Align the needs identified at the Micro level with the Ideal Vision (Mega) and mission (Macro) of your organization.			
Place Micro level needs in a priority order, based on the cost to ignore versus the cost to meet the identified needs.			
Present your Micro level needs to your clients and obtain concurrence.			
List alternative methods and means for addressing your Micro level need(s) and identify the advantages and disadvantages of each.			

Table 7.4. Steps in conducting a Micro level needs assessment.

By collecting valid needs—gaps in results—data, you now have (1) performance criteria for what has to be accomplished and (2) data for calculating value added.

Mega planning and needs assessment are not a linear, rigid, or lock-step approach. Relating Means and Ends (Figure 7.6) is a dynamic—not linear, not lock-step—relationship within an organization. An end, or result, in the development process, might start with a means or activity that in turn delivers another end. Means and ends should be linked, related, and aligned to move increasingly toward Mega as shown again in Figure 7.6.

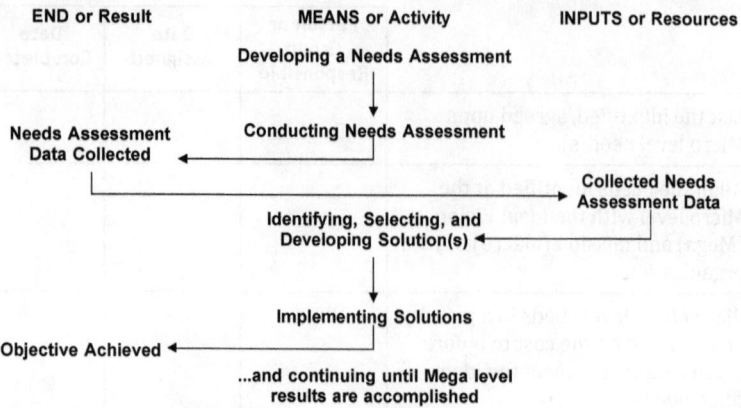

Figure 7.6. The dynamic nature of Means and Ends when doing needs assessment.[14]

Costs and Consequences[15] in the Context of Needs Assessment

An important bonus for using "need" as a noun is that you may derive a reasonable set of indicators for return on investment; estimating what you give and what you get. This is very useful, for you will be likely (if not now, soon) required to justify everything you use, spend, and deliver on the basis of the costs to you and the consequences of what you deliver.

It is difficult to take into account all of the possible costs and the various kinds of consequences, but you can estimate them closely enough to justify what you use, do, produce, and deliver, and to track your costs and returns.

Using an indicator of Mega level consequences.[16] As noted earlier in Chapter 3, an estimate of the societal impact—Mega level consequences—is that an individual's consumption be equal to or less than his or her production:

$$C \leq P$$

where C is consumption as indicated by dollars/money expended by an individual and P is production as indicated by dollars/money obtained by an individual.

Needs and Needs Assessment

This indicator is an approximation of Mega level consequences and payoffs, and it is based on a shorthand definition of Mega level results that no person will be under the care, custody, or control of another person, agency, or substance as indicated by $C \leq P$.

Among the questions that a costs-consequences initiative should answer are:

1. Who are the participants in the interventions? Who should be?
2. Who are being turned down for the interventions? Who should be?
3. What interventions are the participants receiving? What alternative interventions might they receive?
4. What are the results of the intervention or interventions (at the Mega, Macro, and Micro levels)?
5. What are the completion, drop-out, and continuation rates for the participants?
6. What are the performance levels of the completers? What value do they add? What about those who do not complete?
7. What is the societal condition—their levels of self-sufficiency, self-reliance, and quality of life—of the completers? The non-completers? What are the levels of completer's and non-completer's self-sufficiency and self-reliance (in terms, at least, of $C \leq P$)?
8. What interventions and patterns of interventions are making the best contributions in terms of societal (Mega) payoffs and consequences? What is working and what is not? What are the valid criteria for these?
9. What are the societal (Mega) payoffs and consequences for the various interventions for the various kinds of participants (in terms, at least of $C \leq P$)?

10. What are the costs for the payoffs and non-payoffs, and is it worth the expenditures as compared to other interventions that might be made?

11. Have the decisions made not generalized past the completeness and quality of the data?

Using Costs-Consequences Analysis in Any Organization

Using the OEM and the concept of costs-consequences, the following questions allow for the identification of what was missing for useful evaluation and continuous improvement to occur:

- *What data exist?*
- *What data do not exist?*
- *What are critical data required by the project/intervention to determine effectiveness, efficiency, and positive costs-consequences?*
- *What Organizational Elements data exist?*
- *What Organizational Elements data are missing complete and valid data?*
- *Are the gaps between What Is and What Should Be identified?*
- *Are all of the Organizational Elements linked? (Does a "flow" from element to element exist and is it justified?)*

Why do this? It makes sense because when you are required to report on return on investment, or costs-consequences, this provides some guidelines for demonstrating "what you give" and "what you get" for actual or potential interventions. You can provide hard metrics for value added (or value subtracted if things don't go as intended).

The Bernardez Two-Level Business Case Model. Recall that in Chapter 3, Table 3.2, Bernardez's two-level business case (conventional bottom line and societal bottom line) provides an approach to proving value for money. This two bottom lines business case can be very powerful in showing return on investment for both conventional calculations and for societal ones as well. Demonstrating intentions and success can thus be based on demonstrating the cost to meet the needs as compared to the costs for not meeting the needs.

Interestingly, much of what practitioners are advised to do that get called "needs assessments," "needs analyses," "training needs assessments,[17]" and the like are usually *quasi-needs assessments* because they deal with gaps in processes (e.g., training, job aids, methods of supervision, resources desired) and not with results.

Some practical considerations. Needs assessment, as defined here, is a planning process for (a) identifying the gaps between current results and required/desired ones, and (b) placing those needs (gaps in results) in priority order on the basis of the costs to meet the needs as compared to the costs to ignore them. Since a *need* is defined as a gap in results, then there are three types of needs: one each for gaps for *Mega level results*, *Macro level results*, and *Micro level results*.[18] Gaps in non-results, *Processes* and/or *Inputs*, are termed *quasi-needs*. You can do needs assessment at the *Mega*, *Macro*, or *Micro* level by identifying gaps in results for each.

By identifying correct and important needs before implementing any process or solution, you can improve your effectiveness and efficiency. Securing the necessary information for "selecting the right job" in order that doing the job correctly will be fruitful can do this. Often, when dealing with an ongoing system, evaluation data can supply you with the What Is data, but it cannot give you the What Should Be."

Action Steps

1. Needs are gaps in results, not gaps in means or resources. Treat "need" as a noun, not a verb.

2. Before sensibly selecting means and resources, you should know the needs—gaps in results—to be closed. Don't jump to solutions before you know the problems.

3. A useful needs assessment identifies gaps in results at each of three levels of planning and results, and places those needs in priority order on the basis of the cost to meet the need versus the costs to ignore the need. Doing it this way gives you a triple bonus:

   - The What Is part of the assessed needs serves as your objective.

   - The gaps between What Is and What Should Be will provide the basis for evaluation by revealing how much of the need has been reduced or delivered.

   - By using "need" as a gap in results, you can demonstrate the costs of meeting the needs as compared to the costs to ignore the need. This is very powerful for proposals.

4. What commonly gets called a "needs assessment" is usually about gaps in means and resources and might more accurately be called a "solutions assessment."

5. Get commitment of all partners to this approach to needs assessment.

6. A needs assessment should use both perception data (soft data) and performance data (hard data), and you should ensure that both sources of data agree.

7. Don't use a "training needs assessment" even as popular as they are. Research has shown that if you base activities on the basis of that you will be wrong 80 to 90 percent of the time.

8. Stay consistent and rigorous. Use the Six Critical Success Factors constantly.

Endnotes

1. Of course, a dictionary will tell you "need" can be used as a verb. Be warned, however, when you do use it as a verb or in a verb sense you risk jumping into solutions before knowing the real problems, confusing means and ends. The interesting thing about dictionaries is that they give "common usage," not necessarily precise or useful usage. Semantics and words are important, so please give consideration to the specific words and concepts used in this book; the precise use of words are important, even when at first it all seems like semantic quibbling. It is not.

2. Kaufman, R. (1976). *Needs assessment.* San Diego, CA: University Consortium for Instructional Development and Technology.

    Kaufman, R., & English, F. W. (1979). *Needs assessment: Concept and Application.* Englewood Cliffs, NJ: Educational Technology Publications.

    Kaufman, R. (1986a). Obtaining functional results: Relating needs assessment, needs analysis, and objectives. *Educational Technology, 26*(1), pp. 24–27.

    Kaufman, R. (1992). *Strategic planning plus: An organizational guide (revised).* Newbury Park, CA: Sage Publishing.

    Kaufman, R. (1995). *Mapping educational success (revised).* Thousand Oaks, CA: Corwin Press.

    Kaufman, R. (1998). *Strategic thinking: A guide to identifying and solving problems (revised).* Washington, DC and Arlington, VA: The International Society for Performance Improvement and the American Society for Training and Development.

    Kaufman, R. (2000). *Mega planning: Practical tools for organizational success.* Thousand Oaks, CA: Sage Publications. Also *Planificación Mega: Herramientas practicas paral el exito organizacional.* (2004). Traducción de Sonia Agut. Universitat Jaume I, Castelló de la Plana, Espana.

Kaufman, R. (2006a). *Change, choices, and consequences: A guide to Mega Thinking and Planning.* Amherst, MA: HRD Press Inc.

Kaufman, R. (2006b). Seven stupid things people do when they attempt strategic thinking and planning. In Silberman, M., & Phillips, P. *The 2006 ASTD organization development and leadership sourcebook.* Alexandria, VA: ASTD

3. What about Maslow and his 1964 widely revered "Hierarchy of Needs"? Actually, using terms as defined here, Maslow's Hierarchy is actually a hierarchy of "motivators"; it identifies the rough order in which an individual will be motivated to close gaps, from survival to self-actualization. Useful, but not really "needs," but rather motivators.

4. Each of these was mined from published so-called needs assessments. Based on previously published work, including:

   Kaufman, R. (2000). *Mega Planning: Practical tools for organizational success.* Thousand Oaks, CA: Sage Publications. Also *Planificación Mega: Herramientas practicas paral el exito organizacional.* (2004). Traducción de Sonia Agut. Universitat Jaume I, Castelló de la Plana, Espana.

   Kaufman, R. (2006). *Change, choices, and consequences: A guide to Mega Thinking and Planning.* Amherst, MA: HRD Press, Inc.

5. Based in part on Kaufman, R. (2000). *Mega Planning: Practical tools for organizational success.* Thousand Oaks, CA: Sage Publications.

6. Based on Kaufman, R. (1992). *Strategic planning plus: An organizational guide (revised).* Newbury Park, CA: Sage Publishing. and Kaufman, R., Rojas, A. M. & Mayer, H. (1993). Needs assessment: A user's guide. Englewood Cliffs, NJ: *Educational Technology.*

7. Deming, W. E. (1982). *Quality, productivity, and competitive position.* Cambridge, MA: MIT, Center for Advanced Engineering Study.

   Deming, W. E. (1986). *Out of the crisis.* Cambridge, MA: MIT, Center for Advanced Engineering Technology.

   Deming, W. E. (1990: May 10). *A system of profound knowledge.* Washington, DC: Personal memo.

8. Juran, J. M. (1988). *Juran on planning for quality.* New York: The Free Press.

9. Kaufman, R., Thiagarajan, S., & MacGillis, P. (Eds.). (1997). *The guidebook for performance improvement.* San Francisco, CA: Pfeiffer & Co./Division of Jossey-Bass.

   Muir, M., Watkins, R., Kaufman, R., & Leigh, D. (April, 1998). Costs-consequences analysis: A primer. *Performance Improvement, 37*(4), pp. 8–17.

10. Special journal issues on Mega:

    Kaufman, R., & Bernardez, M. (Eds.) (2005) *Performance Improvement Quarterly, 18*(3).

    Kaufman, R., Bernardez, M., & Guerra-Lopez, I. (Eds.) (2009). *Performance Improvement Quarterly.* 22(2).

11. These are based on Chapter 4 of Kaufman, R., & Guerra-Lopez, I. (2008), *The Assessment Book: Applied Strategic Thinking and Performance Improvement through Self-Assessments.* Amherst, MA: HRD Press, Inc., and are truncated here.

12. From other previously cited works by Kaufman.

13. Based on Kaufman, R. (1992). *Strategic planning plus: An organizational guide (revised).* Newbury Park, CA: Sage Publishing, and Kaufman, R., Rojas, A. M., & Mayer, H. (1993). Needs assessment: A user's guide. Englewood Cliffs, NJ: *Educational Technology.*

14. Kaufman, R. (2006). *Change, choices, and consequences: A guide to Mega Thinking and Planning.* Amherst, MA: HRD Press, Inc.

15. This section is based on:

    Kaufman, R. (1998). *Strategic thinking: A guide to identifying and solving problems. (revised).* Washington, D.C., and Arlington, VA: The International Society for Performance Improvement and the American Society for Training and Development.

    Kaufman, R. (2000). *Mega Planning: Practical tools for organizational success.* Thousand Oaks, CA: Sage Publications.

    Oakley-Browne, H., Watkins, R., & Leigh, D. (2003). *Practical strategic planning: aligning people, performance, and payoffs.* San Francisco, CA: Jossey-Bass/Pfeiffer.

    Kaufman, R. (2006). *Change, choices, and consequences: A guide to Mega Thinking and Planning.* Amherst, MA: HRD Press, Inc.

16. Interestingly, most "return on investment" models and procedures leave out Mega. They might reach to customer satisfaction and "contributions," but do not deal with adding measurable value to both external clients and our shared society. In work previously cited by Bernardez, an alternative business case model is now available.

17. Please notice that in my list of important definitions, "training needs assessment" wasn't there. I believe that this is a misnomer for a "training requirements analysis," which is very important *after* you know that training (or some intervention is required). After all, *training* is a means—why would you want to do a needs assessment (determining gaps between current results and desired ones) if you already know that you are going to do training? Again, even the label of one of our favorite tools supplies a bias toward means (training) while assuming that useful ends will surely follow.

18. These three types of results, unfortunately, are not often distinguished in our literature...you would think that "if you've seen one kind of result, you've seen 'em all."

Chapter 8

Implementing the Mega Plan

Applying the Concept and Tools of Mega Thinking and Planning to Measurably Deliver Success

To guide us from inception to demonstrated success, use and apply the basic considerations for Mega Thinking and Planning, the six critical success factors (first noted in Table 4.1):

- Don't assume that what worked in the past will work now. Get out of your comfort zone and be open to change.

- Differentiate between ends (what) and means (how).

- Prepare all objectives (including those for Mega, Macro, and Micro levels) that rigorously state where you are headed and how to tell when you have arrived.

- Define "need" as a gap between current and desired results, not as insufficient levels of means or resources.

- Use and link all three levels of planning and results: Mega/Outcomes, Macro/Outputs, and Micro/Products.

- Use an Ideal Vision (the kind of world we want to create for tomorrow's child stated in measurable terms) as the basis for all thinking and planning: the Mega level.

With these to guide us, start the implementation of strategic thinking and planning, with committing to where our organization should be headed and how to tell when we have arrived. For this, we will use the Ideal Vision to define our mission objective: what parts of the Ideal Vision will we commit to deliver and move ever-closer toward.

Implementation Phase 1: Identify those variables within the Ideal Vision that we commit to deliver and move ever-closer toward. Then, to confirm our selection, we do a needs assessment of the gaps between What Is and What Should Be for those elements. We prioritize those gaps in results on the basis of the costs to meet them as compared to the costs to ignore them.

Implementation Phase 2: Those indicators we commit to delivering based on what we did in #1 becomes our Mission Objective. It states, clearly and rigorously, "where we are headed and how we can measure its accomplishment and track our progress."

Implementation Phase 3: We then do another needs assessment at the Macro level to determine the gaps based on current performance data, select those gaps (needs), and make a listing of the objectives by which we define the organizational functions—clusters of accomplishments—and tasks—performance requirements for individuals. These performance specifications—objectives—provide us with the criteria for

  a. identifying possible ways and means to meet the objectives and the advantages and disadvantages of each possibility;
  b. selecting the most effective and efficient methods and means; and
  c. starting and completing the design, development, implementation, and evaluation and continual improvement/implementation.

Implementing the Mega Plan

As a review, here the Ideal Vision presented earlier is based on "what kind of world do you want to help develop for our children and grandchildren—for tomorrow's child?" Recall, also, that this Ideal Vision is appropriate for any and all organizations in our world: public, private, government, military, non-governmental agency (NGO). Each organization should intend on adding measurable value at the Ideal Vision level. Each organization chooses what elements of the Ideal Vision (Figure 3.1) they commit to add measurable value to and move ever closer toward. Reviewing:

Basic Ideal Vision

The world we want to help create—with others—for tomorrow's child.

There will be no losses of life nor elimination or reduction of levels of survival, self-sufficiency, or quality of life from any source including (but not limited to) the following:

- war, riot, terrorism, or unlawful civil unrest
- unintended human-caused changes to the environment, including permanent destruction of the environment and/or rendering it nonrenewable
- murder, rape, or crimes of violence, robbery, or destruction to property
- substance abuse
- permanent or continuing disabilities
- disease
- starvation and/or malnutrition
- destructive behavior, including child, partner, spouse, self, elder, others
- accidents, including transportation, home, and business/ workplace
- discrimination based on irrelevant variables, including color, race, age, creed, gender, religion, wealth, national origin, or location

---

(continued)

> **Consequences:** Poverty will not exist, and every woman and man will earn at least as much as it costs them to live unless they are progressing toward being self-sufficient and self-reliant. No adult will be under the care, custody, or control of another person, agency, or substance: all adult citizens will be self-sufficient and self-reliant as minimally indicated by their consumption being equal to or less than their production.

The roll-down development, as we move from plans to implementation to measureable success, starts with the Mega/Ideal Vision and then moves to Macro/Mission Objectives to Micro/functions and tasks, and then to implementation:

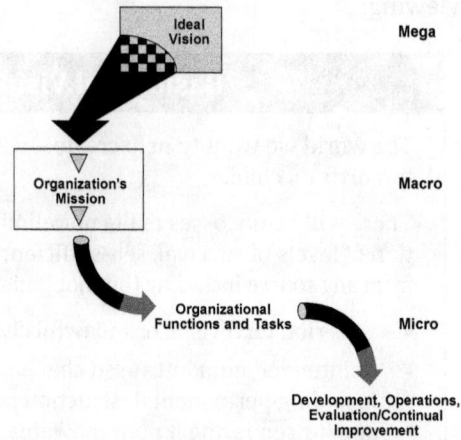

Missions derive from the Ideal Vision. An organization selects what portion of the Ideal Vision it commits to deliver and move ever closer to it.

Implementation Phase 1: Use an Ideal Vision.[1] From this societal-linked Ideal Vision, each organization can identify what part or parts of the Ideal Vision it commits to deliver and move

Implementing the Mega Plan

ever-closer toward.[2] When we base all planning and doing on an Ideal Vision based on the kind of society we want for future generations, we can achieve "strategic alignment" for what we use, do, produce, deliver, and the external payoffs for our Outputs; all of the people and parts of the organization are headed to the same measurable destination and their work can be synergistic, not conflicting.

Based on the elements of the Ideal Vision that an organization commits to deliver and move ever closer to, those become the organization's *mission*.

In order for you to use an Ideal Vision and get the most power from it, here are some guidelines:

- An Ideal Vision is ideal. It defines, in measurable performance terms, the kind of world you and your partners want to create together for tomorrow's child.

- Take the long view; don't be constructed by the here-and-now (or what others are doing).

- Dream. Be idealistic. Imagine a perfect world.[3]

- Don't worry if, at first, a perfect world doesn't seem achievable. You might not be able to get there in your lifetime nor your children's lifetime, but at least you will know where you are headed. You can track your continuous progress. And recall, if you are not headed in that direction, what do you have in mind?

- You and your organization will not be responsible for achieving all of the Ideal Vision, just a part of it.

- Define ends to be accomplished, not means (or resources). Make the ends, or objectives, measurable on an Interval or Ratio scale—measurable indicators of the kind of world you want for your children and grandchildren.

- In writing objectives, including the Ideal Vision, use objectives that state where you are headed and the criteria to be used to track your progress and success.

Each person in the organization, each functional unit in the organization, and the organization itself best moves to achieve Mega. Everyone commits to become one team that chooses adding measurable value to all stakeholders.

For each element in the Ideal Vision, build a matrix with each element listed. Then make sure that at least one of those is used in your strategic, tactical, and operational planning:

Element of the Ideal Vision	Include in Mission Objective
There will be no losses of life nor elimination or reduction of levels of survival, self-sufficiency, or quality of life from any source (including those that follow)	
War, riot, terrorism, or unlawful civil unrest	
Murder, rape, or crimes of violence, robbery, or destruction to property	
Substance abuse	
Permanent or continuing disabilities	
Disease	
Starvation and/or malnutrition	
Destructive behavior (including child, partners, spouse, self, elder, others)	
Accidents, including transportation, home, and business/workplace	
Discrimination, based on irrelevant variables including color, race, age, creed, gender, religion, wealth, national origin, or location	

Implementing the Mega Plan

Doing this will give you a "reality check" to make sure you are thinking and planning Mega and will ensure that your organization has a useful mission.

Implementation Phase 2: Those indicators we commit to delivering based on what we selected in #1 become our mission objective. The mission objective states, clearly and rigorously, "where we are headed and how we can measure its accomplishment and track our progress." Because it links to the Ideal Vision, each person in the organization can plan on how they and their function can contribute to the organization's destination and success.

The mission is accomplished in stages. In operational reality, each organization may set en-route missions as they move for the current What Is in terms of results and value added to internal and external stakeholders to What Should Be. It is useful to develop a "chain of missions" that gives benchmarks for everyone as they move from where they are to where they should be. Figure 8.1 shows a hierarchy of missions, or strategic objectives—each one adding to the next more distant one.

A key to making such useful and practical decisions is to not be limited to each organizational level as specified, but constantly strive to see how close you can come to Mega. Continual improvement at each level will have you continually moving closer to Mega—to the Ideal Vision. It is important to keep in mind that objectives state the minimum, not the maximum: you may exceed an objective.

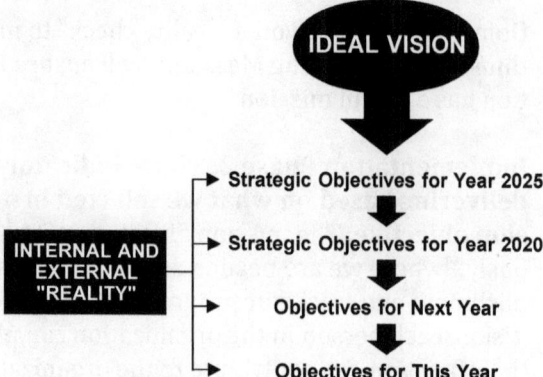

Figure 8.1. A hierarchy of missions.

As you can see in Figure 8.1 above, all lower-level missions cascade down from the Ideal Vision (Mega). Each mission level defines, in measurable terms, what has to be accomplished and delivered on or before the time listed for each.

Implementation Phase 3: We do another needs assessment. We then do another needs assessment at the Macro level to determine the gaps based on current performance data, select those gaps (needs), and make a listing of the objectives by which we define the organizational functions—clusters of accomplishments—and tasks—performance requirements for individuals. These performance specifications—objectives—provide us with the criteria for

    a. identifying possible ways and means to meet the objectives and the advantages and disadvantages of each possibility;

    b. selecting the most effective and efficient methods and means; and

Implementing the Mega Plan

c. starting and completing the design, development, implementation, and evaluation and continual improvement/implementation.

As you implement the Mega plan, it is done in linked phases: each level building upon those above it. This ensures alignment so that everything you use, do, produce, and deliver will add measurable value to external clients and society.

Linking and aligning your progress. As your plan moves down from Mega, there is a linking and overlap between your objectives and plans as you link and align Mega with Macro with Micro and then with Processes and Inputs shown in Figure 8.2.

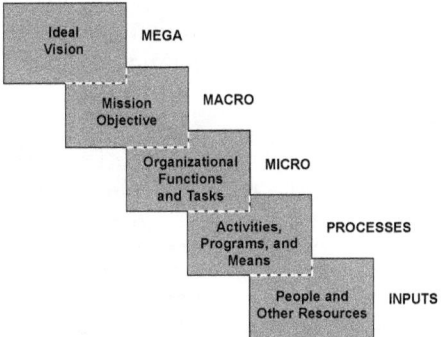

Simultaneity of Planning and Doing: the three levels of planning (Mega, Macro, Micro) and their relation to processes and inputs.

Figure 8.2. The overlap—shown as dotted lines—and flow of moving from Mega to Macro to Micro to Processes to Inputs. There is a linking and overlap as one moves from Mega to Inputs.

Note the overlap from one function to the next. Each lower level builds on the data generated in the level above: a bridge between levels.

135

The Manager's Pocket Guide to Mega Thinking and Planning

Ensuring alignment of everything the organization uses, does, produces, delivers and Mega consequences is important; everyone going to the same place requires cooperative efforts.

In Table 8.1 is an application of that important function. Obtaining alignment can be vital for organizational success in order to ensure that programs, projects, policies, and activities actually complement each other. Using an example of a toaster manufacturer and a suggestion by the chief operating officer for training in product, handling, and shipping, Table 8.1 shows how you may determine alignment by sorting any initiative into the OEM and checking compliance.

MEGA		
Program, Project, and Activity	Policies and Procedures	Law, Rules, and Regulations
(13) Customer satisfaction met as well as documented; zero losses of life, permanent disabilities or reduction of customer well-being from delivered toasters; product line approved by Underwriters Labs for safety.	(14) All products (including the toaster) must have complete safety and have no successful lawsuits or government restrictions or sanctions on any product. Performance data must substantiate these requirements.	(3) Any product must be safe for the purpose intended and meet safety standards of state and federal requirements as well as those in foreign countries where marketed.
MACRO		
(12) Toasters, packaging, instructions, and warranty materials are shipped to customers as promised.	(4) Any suggested training program has to be approved by production manager and program manager and will meet needs at the Mega, Macro, and Micro levels.	Any human intervention must meet federal and state employment requirements.

(continued)

Implementing the Mega Plan

	MICRO	
Program, Project, and Activity	**Policies and Procedures**	**Law, Rules, and Regulations**
(5) Managers approve training program based on needs—gaps in performance—and value added at Mega and Macro levels.	(10) Toaster production quality is tested and certified. (11) Toasters are packed and ready for sending to shipping for delivery.	
	PROCESS	
(1) Training is recommended by COO for toaster production. (7) Performance improvement experiences (training) are designed, developed, formatively evaluated. (8) Competent toaster production personnel are certified. (9) Toaster production is implemented.		
	INPUT	
(6) Existing SKAAs for potential trainees are identified. Operational environment, including workplace requirements, is identified and approved.	(2) Training must be based on a needs assessment and produce measurable SKAAs that add internal and external value.	

Table 8.1. Alignment table used for a potential product and a suggested intervention—a training program (with the sequence of steps numbered).

In this example, the sequence of events and functions are noted with numbers (1) through (14) to show the order in which a new potential initiative (toaster production and possible associated training) may be sorted into the Organizational Elements Model, and alignment with policies and procedures (Column 3) as well as laws, rules, and regulations (Column 4) is checked and ensured.

When considering any program, project, or activity, sort it into the OEM—Table 2.1—and see where it fits. Then make sure that its successful completion will link and align all the organizational elements. Table 8.1 provides an example for a possible training program being considered for a new toaster and its production. The starting point in the alignment-assurance process starts with (1) in the Table 8.1 process cell. Then the alignment check goes forward. Follow the numbers to see the hypothetical flow; successful transfer of skills, knowledge, attitudes, and abilities (SKAAs) should add value to that product as it moves from within the organization to a safe and useful consumer item. By placing toaster production training in the alignment table, you may observe what is possibly missing and what has to be accomplished in order to ensure linkage and to make sure that what you use, do, produce, and deliver will add value both within the organization and outside of it.

As you implement, you move into Implementation Phase 2 by doing a needs assessment first at the Mega level and then subsequently at the Macro and then Micro levels.

The steps for conducting a needs assessment were provided earlier:

Mega level needs assessment: Table 7.2
Macro level needs assessment: Table 7.3
Micro level needs assessment: Table 7.4

Collecting and Displaying Needs Assessment Data

Table 8.2 is a useful way of summarizing and presenting needs assessment data. Note that, as suggested throughout, you ensure that there is always alignment among Mega, Macro, and Micro.

Implementing the Mega Plan

Take the following steps to summarize and present needs assessment data using the Needs Assessment Summary Format:

1. Collect the needs (gaps in results) data and enter it into the Needs Assessment Summary Format. Then for each, confirm that:
   a. Each stated need identifies a need as a gap in results, then
   b. For each process or resources-referenced statement in column 2 (that some people might at first mislabel as a "need"), ask "If we were successful at this, what would be the result?" Thus, convert any quasi-need (a gap in methods or a gap in resources) into a need, and then
2. For each need identified, classify it as:

   Mega/Outcomes-related
   Macro/Outputs-related
   Micro/Products-related

   Note the needs listed for each results level. Anything missing? Are there needs for Mega, Macro, and Micro? Are they linked and aligned? If not, collect more data to ensure linkage.
3. List the needs and obtain approval of your planning partners.

Current Results	Possible Means	Required Results	Related Ideal Vision Element	Need Level Focus		
				Mega	Macro	Micro

Figure 8.2. Needs assessment summary format.

Implementing the Mega Plan

Using the What Is and What Should Be Format for Collecting Data

An advantage of using *need* as a noun—gap in results—is that you can use the What Is and What Should Be format to collect useful data and define gaps in results all at the same time. Use the following scale to indicate your level of agreement with each statement:

SA – Strongly Agree
A – Agree
N – Neutral
D – Disagree
SD – Strongly Disagree

WHAT IS						WHAT SHOULD BE			
SA	A	N	D	SD	STATEMENT (Results-Related*)	SA	A	N	SD
					1. This organization is client centered.				
					2. Our performance objectives are written in measurable performance terms.				
					3. We plan to deliver value at the Mega level.				
					4. Results, not politics, are rewarded here.				
					5. Evaluation is conducted at the three levels of results: Mega, Macro, and Micro.				
					6. Minority employment policies are attracting and keeping competent and productive people.				
					7. We learn from our mistakes.				
					8. Personnel/HRD policies encourage individual productivity.				
					9. Resources are available when required.				

WHAT IS				STATEMENT (Results-Related*)	WHAT SHOULD BE			
SA	A	N	D	SD		SA	A	N	D	SD

					STATEMENT (Results-Related*)					
					10. Resources are of proper quality.					
					11. Deliveries are on time.					
					12. All deliveries meet customer requirements.					
					13. There are zero customer complaints.					
					14. Associates are 100% competent in all skills, knowledge, attitudes, and abilities.					
					15. There are no deaths or disabilities from what we deliver.					
					16. Our workplace is completely safe.					
					17. There are no negative environmental impacts from our work and activities.					
					18. Everyone understands the Mission of our organization.					
					19. All associates make a contribution to their work assignment, the organization's Outputs, external clients' success, and societal well-being.					
					20. Etc.					

*Mixed Mega, Macro, and Micro results

Implementing the Mega Plan

This format—based on a needs assessment approach—is very useful for collecting data and ensuring that the data collection identifies gaps between current results and desired results. Because this type of data collection is "soft" or observational data, it is strongly urged that such be compared to "hard" performance data.

How do needs assessments you have used or know about stack up with the requirements for delivering useful data? The following could be useful when you are considering a needs assessment you have been involved in, or looking at one that has been used before.

Using a needs assessment you have developed or recall being used:

Compare your needs assessment and determine if it includes:

❏ 1a. Mega level data,

❏ 1b. Macro level data, and/or

❏ 1c. Micro level data.
(It might be that it is "none of the above").

Note: A way to determine if it is Mega (societal) focused is to determine if elements of an Ideal Vision (Figure 3.1) are included.

❏ 2. Does your needs assessment focus on ends and not means?

❏ 3. What are the implications for your internal (organizational) and external clients' success that will be delivered by the needs assessment you are comparing relative with this (Mega) approach and this exercise?

❏ 4. Does your needs assessment use a combination of "hard" and "soft" data? Is this data collected from a variety of data sources throughout the organization?

Follow-on questions:

5. If the needs assessment does not include a Mega level focus or links, what will it take to modify it?
6. What are the penalties and payoffs for you and your internal and external clients for using a Mega-level-linked needs assessment? For not using a Mega-level-linked needs assessment?
7. Why do you think most needs assessment models and frameworks don't include or link to the Mega level?

Moving from Mega to Macro to Micro to Processes to Inputs: Solving problems. It is not enough to identify and prioritize needs, nor is it enough to just identify the requirements for success—for change. While not the topic of this book[4], Figure 8.3 shows the functions, or steps, required to get from "here" to "there"—to deliver success[5].

Mega Thinking and Planning is about defining a shared success, achieving it, and being able to prove it. Mega Thinking and Planning is a focus not on one's organization alone but on society now and in the future. It is about adding measurable value to all stakeholders.

Implementing the Mega Plan

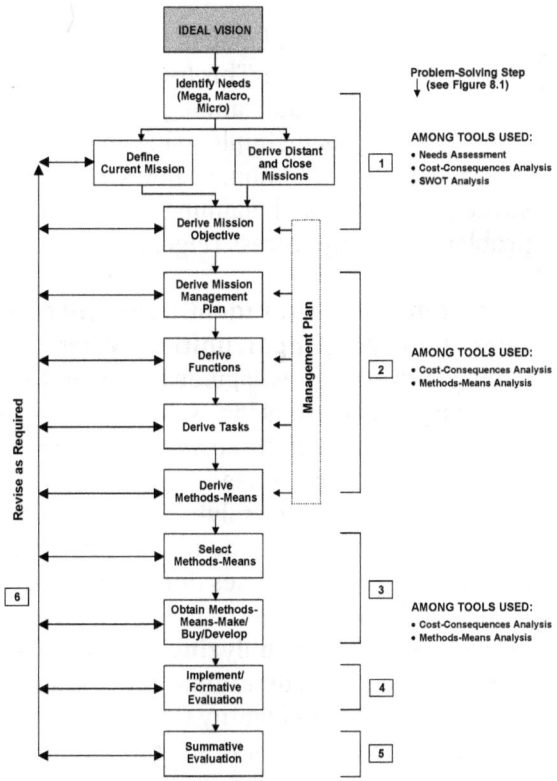

Figure 8.3. A relationship map of Mega Thinking and Planning, and doing: Relating tools and concepts.[6]

Use the conceptual map in Figure 8.3 as a guide for Mega Thinking and Planning. This framework relates the functions for strategic thinking and planning—from the Ideal Vision through design, development, implementation, and evaluation/continual improvement. In addition, it shows how each phase of the strategic thinking and planning cycle relates to the six-step problems-solving process (Figure 8.4).

A six-step process for identifying and resolving problems (and identifying opportunities). When progressing, the following six functions will guide you to perform. They start with assessing needs—gaps in results—and placing them in priority order on the basis of the costs to meet the needs as compared to the costs to ignore the needs.

A six-step problem-solving process model, shown in Figure 8.4, in terms of results (and not the processes to deliver each result) includes (1.0) **assessing needs,** which defines the gaps in results at the Mega, Macro, and Micro levels and places them in priority order; (2.0) **analyzing needs** (gaps in results) to find the causes of the needs, determine detailed solution requirements to meet the needs, and identify (but not yet select) solution alternatives; (3.0) **selecting methods and means,** which involve selecting solutions from among alternatives based on the costs and consequences for the available alternatives; (4.0) **implementing,** which consists of designing and developing the means and methods that are required to meet the needs, and then putting those to work; (5.0) **evaluating,** where the results are compared with the intentions (from 2.0); and (6.0) **revising as required,** which involves the continual improvement (at each and every step) when the required results are not being accomplished or when progress toward meeting the needs is falling short.

Implementing the Mega Plan

The Six-Step Problem-Solving Process

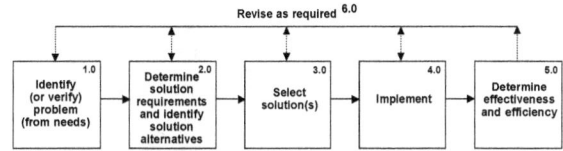

Figure 8.4. The six-step problem solving process: A process for identifying and resolving problems (and identifying opportunities).[7]

This problem-solving process will allow you to manage the entire planning and change process. It suggests the steps that start with

- 1.0, identifying a problem from a needs assessment, to
- 2.0, determining solution requirements and identifying alternative methods and means for meeting the needs, then
- 3.0, selecting the most effective methods and means, to
- 4.0, implementing what was planned and designed, to
- 5.0, evaluation of what worked and what did not.

There is the continuous and dynamic "revise as required" step—6.0—that encourages revising whenever and wherever proper progress is not being made.

Putting Everything to Work

It is now time to apply the concepts, models, processes, and tools provided in Chapters 1-8. Rather than have you go back and search each time, critical figures will be repeated here, in the context of applications.

When defining where to go and justifying why you want to go there, use the basic steps provided earlier in the context of change, choices, and consequences; your decisions, your results, your consequences:

- The Ideal Vision—Mega, where to head,
- The Organizational Elements Model—what are the linked three levels of results and what are the methods and resources to use,
- The Six Critical Success Factors—making sure you get to where you should go.

To guide your actions from concept to application to success is:

- The Six-Step Problem-Solving Process—for finding and implementing the best ways and means to get from here to there.

Know what not to do as well as what to do. In addition to knowing the right things to use and do, you can also benefit from knowing what not to do—choosing what is useful, not simply what is conventional. We can count on change happening: we can take control or wait for things to happen to us. We may be proactive or reactive. Be proactive.

Business cases and Mega Thinking and Planning. In most organizational activities, one is expected to provide a "business case." Business cases, at their best, identify and document the relationship between what is spent (time, money, resources) and what benefits are derived for the organization in the short run. Business cases usually stop at Macro—the payoffs for the organization—and usually relate to payoffs in immediate fiscal quarters or immediate years.

As sensible as this might seem at first, conventional business plans almost always fail to formally factor in the value added to external clients and society. Because they do not include Mega, they are incomplete. It is risky to base any plan, including a business plan, only on return-on-investment/return-on-equity for the organization alone.

Use the cost–consequences information and procedures provided in Chapter 3. This is vital for you to demonstrate value added.

Implementing the Mega Plan

A Management Plan for Mega Thinking and Planning

Figure 8.5 provides a flow chart, or management plan, for Mega Thinking and Planning.

After the decision to Mega plan,

1.0 Identify the parts of the Ideal Vision you commit to deliver and move ever closer toward, and at the same time

2.0 Overcome cultural and individual elements that block useful planning and change, then

3.0 Identify the Mission Objective that states, in measurable terms, where you are headed and the criteria for measuring progress and if you have arrived, then

4.0 Identify functions to be accomplished: what building block results have to be completed within your organization to get from What Is to What Should Be, then

5.0 Identify possible methods-means (tactics, tools, approaches, programs, activities), and then

6.0 Select the methods-means identified in 5.0 (perhaps using costs-consequences tools to project possible impact and value added), and then

7.0 Implement the methods-means and track the progress based on the performance criteria derived for each function and task, and then

8.0 Determine the effectiveness and efficiency so that you will continually improve. This step of continually improving actually goes on at all times; at any point in the management plan when accomplishments don't meet the requirements, revise then and there.

In the lower part of this figure are listed some of the basic resources required for successful Mega Thinking and Planning.

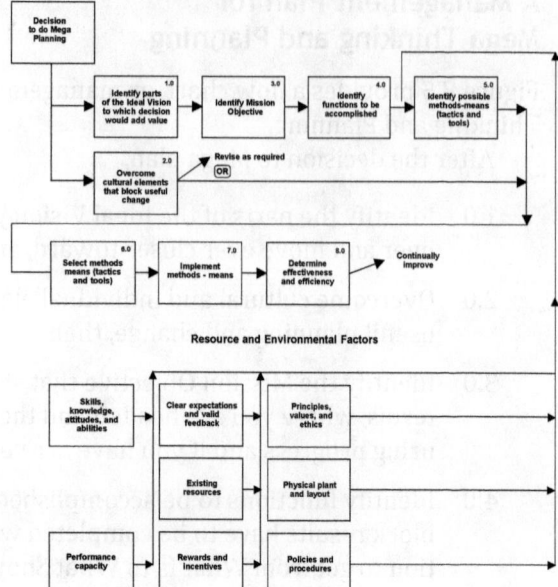

Figure 8.5. A management plan for Mega Thinking and Planning.

Implementing the Mega Plan

> **Action Steps**
>
> 1. Apply the three guides and do that consistently and with the rigor involved.
> 2. Don't "go native" and fall back into the conventional methods used by others for strategic planning and needs assessment. It might be more comfortable at first but it will not lead to your success.
> 3. The tools and techniques provided in this book will serve you well. Use them.

Endnotes

1. Kaufman, R. (2006). *Change, choices, and consequences: A guide to Mega Thinking and Planning.* Amherst, MA: HRD Press, Inc.

2. Based on Kaufman, R. (1998). *Strategic thinking: A guide to identifying and solving problems (revised).* Washington, DC and Arlington, VA: The International Society for Performance Improvement and the American Society for Training and Development.

3. All organizations, public and private, have the same Ideal Vision. Each organization is responsible for adding measurable value to our shared communities and society.

4. Many so-called "needs assessment" models exist. Not all really deal with needs. There are a number of so-called needs assessment models and processes available. The question any adopter should ask is "How many of the Organizational Elements are vital to my success?" A comparison of various popular models of so-called and actual needs assessments may be found in:

   Leigh, D., Watkins, R., Platt, W., and Kaufman, R. (2000). Alternate models of needs assessment: A digest, review, and comparison of needs assessment literature. *Human Resource Development Quarterly, 11*(1), pp. 87–93.

Watkins, R., Leigh, D., Platt, W., & Kaufman, R. (1998). Needs assessment: A digest, review, and comparison of needs assessment literature. *Performance Improvement, 37*(7), pp. 40–53.

Watkins, R., Leigh, D., & Kaufman, R. (1999). Choosing a needs assessment model. In Silberman, M. *Team and Organizational Development Sourcebook.* New York: McGraw Hill.

5. Information on "system analysis" tools is provided in:

   Kaufman, R. (1998). *Strategic thinking: A guide to identifying and solving problems (revised).* Washington, DC and Arlington, VA: The International Society for Performance Improvement and the American Society for Training and Development. (Recipient of the 2001 International Society for Performance Improvement "Outstanding Instructional Communication Award.") Also, Spanish edition, *El Pensamiento Estrategico.* Centro de Estudios: Roman Arces, S.A., Madrid, Spain.

   Kaufman, R. (2000). *Mega Planning: Practical tools for organizational success.* Thousand Oaks, CA: Sage Publications. Also *Planificación Mega: Herramientas practices paral el exito organizacional.* (2004). Traducción de Sonia Agut. Universitat Jaume I, Castelló de la Plana, Espana.

   Kaufman, R., Oakley-Browne, H., Watkins, R., & Leigh, D. (2003). *Practical strategic planning: Aligning people, performance, and payoffs.* San Francisco, CA: Jossey-Bass/Pfeiffer.

6. An original version of this was developed by Dr. Ingrid Guerra-Lopez as part of a presentation on Mega Planning for The Center for Needs Assessment and Planning. Florida State University.

7. Kaufman, R. (1992). *Strategic planning plus: An organizational guide (revised).* Newbury Park, CA: Sage Publishing.

Kaufman, R. (1998). *Strategic thinking: A guide to identifying and solving problems (revised).* Washington, D.C., and Arlington, VA: The International Society for Performance Improvement and the American Society for Training and Development.

Kaufman, R. (2000). *Mega Planning: Practical tools for organizational success.* Thousand Oaks, CA: Sage Publications.

Kaufman, R. (2006). *Change, choices, and consequences: A guide to Mega Thinking and Planning.* Amherst, MA: HRD Press, Inc.

Chapter 9

Evaluation and Continual Improvement: What Worked, What Didn't, What to Keep, and What to Change

Evaluation: Different Yet Related to Needs Assessment

Needs assessment and evaluation are related but not the same. Let's take a look at how they are related, how they are different, and how both are key to successful planning and doing: Planning is proactive; it seeks to define and achieve a useful future.

- Evaluation is reactive; it finds what worked and what did not.
- Evaluation compares results with intentions.
- Evaluation is after-the-fact. Needs assessment and planning is before-the-fact.
- Evaluation data should be used ONLY for fixing and improving, NEVER for blaming.
- The basics of evaluation are not complex, but you might think so from the literature and all of the "cult followings" and rituals.
- Evaluation data—comparing "what was accomplished" with "what was intended" is best used for continuous improvement. *Continual improvement* is the process for changing what should be changed whenever you realize that a change is required.
- Evaluation should use two kinds of data: "hard" and "soft." Hard data are independently verifiable, and soft data are personal and based on perception. Make sure that both kinds of data agree.

- Needs assessments should also include both hard and soft data, but these data only relate to finding the gaps between current results and desired ones.
- When Mega is considered in evaluation, it is called "Evaluation Plus" to indicate that it goes beyond conventional evaluation frameworks.

Needs assessment and evaluation: different but related. Both needs assessment and evaluation deal with gaps, but for different purposes. Needs assessments and evaluation are related but different.

When you do *needs assessment*, you are, before the fact, finding the gaps between current results and desired ones: a comparison of What Is with What Should Be or "could be." Evaluation is reactive, needs assessment is proactive.

When you *evaluate* you compare, after-the-fact, the results that were obtained with the results you intended to accomplish: a comparison of what was accomplished with what was intended.

Needs assessment and evaluation pose different yet related questions. Both compare intended with actual results, but evaluation is always after-the-fact—comparing results with intentions—while a needs assessment proactively identifies the gaps between current results and desired results.

Needs assessment data provide the criteria for evaluation, and evaluation provides the data about what was actually accomplished and delivered.

Because the two are related (and often confused in conventional usage), let's take a closer look at the relative of needs assessment: evaluation.

Figure 9.1 provides a tool for guiding you in evaluation and continual improvement.

Evaluation and Continual Improvement

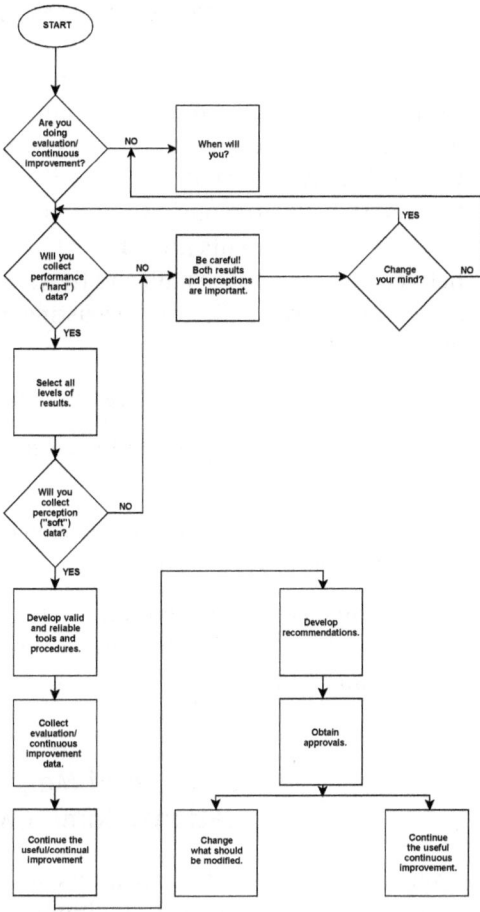

Figure 9.1. A job aid for deciding on what to do for evaluation and continual improvement.

Proactive and reactive tools: Needs assessment and evaluation.
Needs assessment is a *proactive* planning tool, and is distinct from evaluation. Evaluation is a retrospective, or after-the-fact, concern with gaps between what was achieved through our efforts and the targets we have previously set for ourselves.

Needs assessments are forward looking and determine gaps between our current results and those we *should* obtain. Needs assessments are not limited to existing objectives, but may be used in deriving new ones.

- Evaluation compares results with intentions.
- Evaluation is after-the-fact. Needs assessment and planning is before-the-fact.
- Evaluation data should be used *only* for fixing and improving, *never* for blaming.
- The basics of evaluation are not complex, but you might think so from the literature and all of the "cult followings" and rituals.

Evaluation of Mega Planning Applications: Some Cases in Point

There are a number of applications of Mega Thinking and Planning in most parts of our world ranging from Australia, New Zealand, Canada, Central America, South America, to Europe and Asia. Practical applications include the Australian Department of Defense, New Zealand Army, U.S. Coast Guard, and the government of Panama, among others.

Specific uses include African Women's health, public employee union and management collective bargaining, vocational rehabilitation, and social change.[1]

The following three specific cases provide examples and performance data from which we can learn and that demonstrate the viability of the approach.

The Refinor Case

Argentina was home to a major gas production and distribution company. YPF, that was privatized and purchased by Refinor. Mariona Bernardez became the key management consultant who applied Mega Thinking and Planning to that operation to ensure it was a viable business as well as dealing with its social and human resources obligations. With successful implementation, Refinor was sold to Petrobras who went back to conventional bottom line thinking and management. Bernardez traced key indicators for (a) hours of social work invested in community projects, (b) market share of the regional fuel market, (c) local unemployment rate, (d) riots, incidents, and disruptions reported by the police, and (e) property loss.

Data in Figure 9.2 show that indicators during the application of Mega improved during that time period, but was wanting before and after Mega.

Strategic Performance Indicators (SPI)

Indicator (SPI)	Definition
Hours of social work	Hour of social work included the time invested in community projects by the company and volunteers
Market share	Refinor's share of the regional fuel market
Local unemployment rate	As defined by statistics from INDEC and government of Salta for Aguaray, Pocitos, Tartagal, and Mosconi, the main communities surrounding Refinor's refinery and main infrastructure.
Riots and incidents	As reported by local police
Property loss	As reported by local authorities

(continued)

The Manager's Pocket Guide to Mega Thinking and Planning

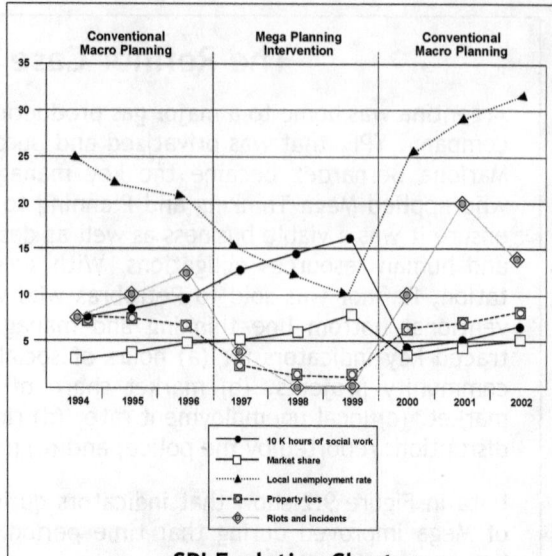

SPI Evolution Chart

Figure 9.2. Data relative to an organization shifting to Mega Thinking and Planning and then back again. The societal contributions and impact are severally addressed.

This is a before, during, and after assessment of the application of Mega Thinking and Planning.

Evaluation and Continual Improvement

The Sonora (Mexico) Institute of Technology

Almost two decades ago, the management and faculty of a technical university adopted societal value added and wealth creation for the entire organization. They went through several phases, Planning, Implementation, Evaluation of Curricular Results, Evaluation of Social Impact, and Evaluation of innovation and leadership. Now six campuses, they adopted an Ideal Vision and mission and also created a Ph.D. and an MBA in performance improvement. As they progressed, they also created more than a dozen incubator projects (such as a Software Factory) that, using Mega, developed viable businesses. The university has been recognized as one of the innovative institutions of higher learning in Mexico and recognized by the president of Mexico and now has the choice to continue to be innovate and practical.

Proposed Transformation of a Major Central American City[2]

The second largest city in Panama has struggled while the capital had developed and prospered. A team was invited by the executive of this country to demonstrate how Mega Thinking and Planning could transform the city that was in crisis. The proposed business case and rationale follow in Figure 9.3.

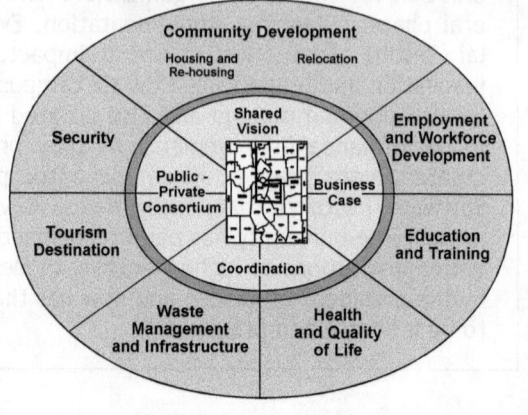

Evaluation and Continual Improvement

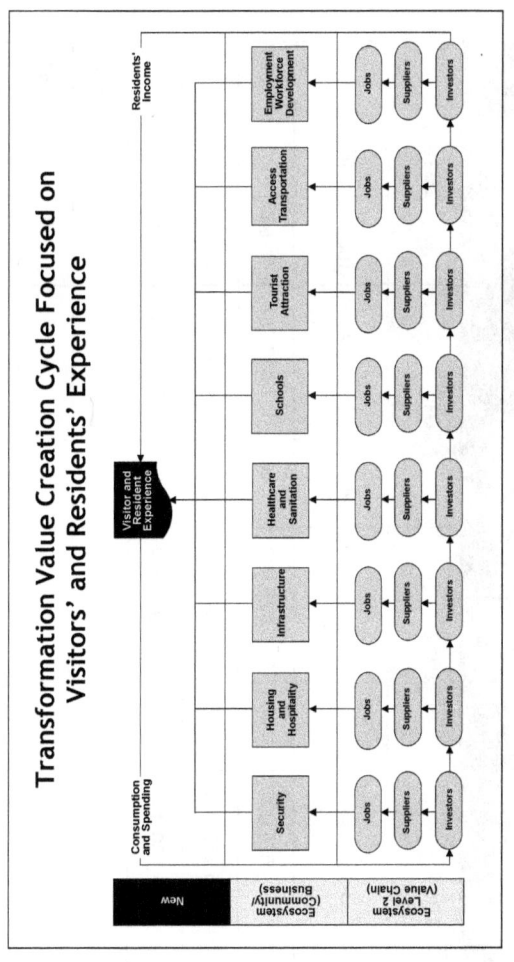

(continued)

NEW - BUSINESS CASE

MEGA LEVEL RESULTS (SOCIAL IMPACT)	2011		2012		2013		2014	
	Jobs	Income	Jobs	Income	Jobs	Income	Jobs	Income
Relocation	60	576,000	60	576,000	60	117,782	60	117,782
Redevelopment (Demo Block)	409	5,265,009	818	7,848,960	1,123	14,465,895	2,044	26,325,044
Tourism	80	1,030,334	160	2,060,669	192	2,472,803	230	2,967,363
Hotels and restaurants	80	768,000	128	1,228,800	192	1,474,560	184	1,769,472
Waste management	80	235,565	160	471,129	192	565,355	230	452,284
Shipping Terminals	100 50	960,000 480,000	200 84	1,920,000 806,400	240 101	471,129 197,874	288 121	565,355 237,449
Free zone	15	242,375	20	192,000	30	58,891	36	70,669
Infrastructure	60	176,673	90	864,000	135	265,010	162	318,012
Private and public projects (click for detail)	545	5,232,000	545	5,232,000	545	5,232,000	545	5,232,000

(continued)

Evaluation and Continual Improvement

MEGA LEVEL RESULTS (SOCIAL IMPACT) (cont'd.)	2011		2012		2013		2014	
	Jobs	Income	Jobs	Income	Jobs	Income	Jobs	Income
Government								
Police/Security	120	1,152,000	240	2,304,000	360	706,694	432	848,033
Justice	60	576,000	120	1,152,000	180	353,347	216	424,016
Education	80	768,000	160	1,536,000	240	471,129	288	565,355
Health cost reduction		3,812,629		4,575,155		5,490,186		6,588,223
Unemployment cost reduction		13,464,334,		6,028,806		4,320,644		4,762,757
Crime & security cost reduction		2,186,486		3,498,377		4,198,052		5,037,663
TOTAL MEGA RESULTS	**1,739**	**36,925,405**	**2,785**	**40,294,296**	**3,590**	**40,861,353**	**4,837**	**56,281,478**

(continued)

	2011		2012		2013		2014	
MACRO LEVEL RESULTS (BUSINESS IMPACT)	Jobs	Income	Jobs	Income	Jobs	Income	Jobs	Income
Tourism revenue	1.2	974,115		1,948,230		6,823,916		8,188,699
Real estate revenue		10,656,050		21,312,100		42,624,200		53,280,250
Construction revenue		77,432,318		65,811,040		58,581,312		44,999,161
Waste management revenue		942,259		1,884,517		2,261,421		1,809,137
Terminals								
Free zone								
Estimated tax revenue								
TOTAL MACRO RESULTS		90,004,741		90,955,887		110,290,849		108,277,247

(continued)

Evaluation and Continual Improvement

MICRO LEVEL RESULTS (DELIVERABLES)	2011 Jobs	2011 Income	2012 Jobs	2012 Income	2013 Jobs	2013 Income	2014 Jobs	2014 Income
Jobs created (City+Dem block)	1,739		2,785		3,590		4,837	
Housing units built/remodeled	583		583		1,165		2,330	
Tourist visits (City+Demo block)	34,906		92,448		154,080		308,160	
City	34,560		77,040		128,400		256,800	
Demo Block	346		15,408		25,680		51,360	
Training and workforce devel.	1,739		2,785		3,590		4,837	
Security (total crime)								
Infrastructure Water								
Power								
Lights								

(continued)

MICRO LEVEL RESULTS (DELIVERABLES)	2011		2012		2013		2014	
	Jobs	Income	Jobs	Income	Jobs	Income	Jobs	Income
Clean air, environment								
Unemployment rate	23.7		17		14		11.85	
Total unemployed	8,087		5,801		4,777		4,044	
Reduction per year	2,286		1,024		734		809	
COSTS	2011		2012		2013		2014	
Program planning, integration, and coordination		400,000		300,000		250,000		200,000
Redevelopment cost		16,700,000		8,350,000		6,680,000		5,010,000
Housing and relocation cost		9,000,000		9,000,000		9,000,000		9,000,000
Tourism investment								
Training and workforce development		2,972,200		1,330,836		953,766		1,051,360

(continued)

Evaluation and Continual Improvement

COSTS (cont'd.)	2011		2012		2013		2014	
Security development cost								
Waste management cost		942,259		1,884,517		2,261,421		1,809,137
Infrastructure investment		57,750,000		57,750,000		57,750,000		57,750,000
TOTAL COSTS	0	87,764,459	0	78,615,353	0	76,895,186	0	74,820,497
CONVENTIONAL BOTTOM LINE (MACRO-COSTS)		2,240,282		12,340,534		33,395,663		33,456,750
SOCIETAL BOTTOM LINE (MEGA + MACRO - COSTS)		39,165,687		52,634,830		74,257,015		89,738,228
VALUE CREATION RATIO (SOCIETAL/CONVENTIONAL)		17.5		4.3		2.2		2.7

Figure 9.3. Applying Mega Thinking and Planning to the transformation of a city and applying the Bernardez 2-level business case, projects that a positive return-on-investment—if the initiative is management completely—could start in the first year.

> This application integrates the many aspects of a city and community and considers them as a whole—as a system—in identifying the costs and consequences of all variables, not just one or a few. Such Mega Thinking and Planning can offer options not usually recognized in programs of planned change and transformation.
>
> These examples provide justification of why Mega Thinking and Planning is valid and useful. The example here shows the power of this holistic approach that Mega Thinking and Planning takes. It is "a system approach" because it considers all of the variables on the entire system instead of just focusing on one or two subsystems. Because all of the subsystems do interact, this takes that dynamic relationship into account. It makes the likelihood of delivering success and proving it a reality.

Mega Thinking and Planning works. It may be successfully applied in a wide range of areas in the public as well as private sectors. It can define and deliver success and add value—measurable value—to all stakeholders.

Action Steps

1. Realize that Mega Thinking and Planning as well as needs assessment are proactive. They are used to create a future based on hard evidence.

2. Realize the evaluation, as important as it is, is reactive. You can only evaluate what has happened.

3. Both needs assessment and evaluation use the same data: the gaps between current results and desired results.

4. Use evaluation data only for fixing and never for blaming.

5. Evaluation is based on data—data from the gaps between What Is and What Should Be.

6. Mega Thinking and Planning has been successful in a wide range of applications, cultures, and organizations, so use with confidence.

Endnotes

1. Kaufman, R., & Bernardez, M. (Eds.) (2005). Special issue on using societal value added as the practical alternative to conventional failure. *Performance Improvement Quarterly, 18*(3), and Kaufman, R., Bernardez, M., & Guerra-Lopez, I. (2009). (Eds.). Special invited issue on Mega planning. *Performance Improvement Quarterly, 22*(2).

2. Developed by Mariano Bernardez in response to a cabinet level request to a team comprised of Carmen Arias, Adam Krivatsy, Mariano Bernardez, and Roger Kaufman for a business case for the application of Mega planning to transform the entire city of Colon.

Chapter 10

Some Final Guidance

When you use Mega Thinking and Planning, following are some guidelines to assist you.

Some Rules of the Mega Thinking and Planning Road[1]

1. *Professionals are responsible for not only what they do, but also the consequences of what they deliver. Results and value added are the coin of the professional realm. If you—or anyone else—do less than deliver useful results, there is an ethics problem.*

   Application guides: (a) Act as if you will read about what you did and accomplished in tomorrow's newspaper[2] or act as if you had to appear in court tomorrow and prove—using the strict rules of scientific and evaluative evidence—that what you did and delivered was effective; (b) never do anything simply for the money or to please someone else if you know what you are doing will not achieve the goal; and (c) continually improve. Use performance data for fixing and never for blaming.

2. *There are three linked levels of planning—Mega, Macro, and Micro[3]—and three associated (and linked) levels of results—Outcomes, Outputs, and Products.[4] Mega focuses on society as the primary client and beneficiary—societal value added—and measures results called Outcomes. Macro focuses on the organization itself as the primary client and beneficiary and measures results called Outputs. Micro focuses on individuals and small groups and measures results called Products.*

   Application guides: (a) Link everything you deliver to the value it will add within and outside of the organization; (b) organizations must be treated as a system, not a loose confederation of isolated subsystems; (c) if what you use, do, produce, and deliver does not add value within as well as outside of the total organization, don't do it; (d) people's impressions and observations are useful, but they must be substantiated with hard performance data. If the two don't agree, work together, using facts and data, until they do agree.

3. *Use the extensive literature that improves every year—including scientific studies of how people learn, master required performance, and actually perform—to determine and justify what you use, produce, and deliver.*

   Application guides: (a) Use scientific information, methods, and tools for designing, delivering, and revising any intervention. Science is based on defining and testing hypotheses. If there is no scientific proof, be skeptical. (b) Look for existing tests and evaluation data for the products or services you want to implement. It is likely that someone has already done part of your work for you. (c) Behavior is not the same as performance. Define the performance you want then identify the behaviors that will deliver the performance. Then identify ways and means to get both the behavior and performance. The growing field of *evidence-based management*, like the same approach in medicine, fits well with Mega Thinking and Planning in that decisions are best made on the basis of solid research evidence and performance data.

4. *Define needs as gaps in results, not as deficiencies in resources or methods.*

   Application guides: (a) Prioritize needs on the basis of the cost to meet the need as compared to the cost to ignore them; (b) focus on results before selecting means and resources; (c) needs assessment ≠ needs analysis, ends ≠ means, and needs ≠ wants; (d) if you start performance improvement at the individual performance level and without linking that to internal and external performance contributions, you will be wrong—if you believe Deming and Juran—80 to 90 percent of the time; (e) select resources and methods on the basis of that which will meet the needs at the least cost in time, money, and human resources. Look for positive costs-consequences that show "what you give" as compared to "what you get"—costs-consequences.

5. *Major resistance to change is usually based on fear: fear of not knowing how well the change will be accepted, fear of not knowing how to implement the change, fear of finding out what one doesn't want to know.*

    Application guides: (a) Change is painful for most people. The less the discomfort from change, the more trivial it may be. (b) Useful change is not usually incremental: it often happens in large leaps and when you find the right incentives, change can be quick. (c) Be proactive. If you wait for things to happen so you can react, you will always be trying to catch up. Define the kind of world you want to help create for tomorrow's person and then contribute to that. (d) Systematic planning helps reduce the pain and the fear in change situations. (e) Don't attack a person for their fear—help them. (f) Use evaluation data for improving and not for blaming.

6. *Don't trust any solution that will fit on a bumper sticker. Short and snappy might be appealing, but don't lose the rigor and precision in order to get acceptance.*

You might have some more to add. The important thing is that we deal in scientifically based results and add value inside and outside of the organization. If you don't have that in mind, what do you intend to do to prove you are a professional?

Here is a list of the seven stupid things people do when they do conventional strategic planning:[5]

1. Call all levels of planning "strategic" and thus not aligning societal value-added (Mega), organizational contributions (Macro), and individual performance contributions (Micro).
2. Confuse ends and means and blur strategy, tactics, operations, and methods and assume that there are just some things that "are not measurable."
3. Base strategic plans only on perceptions, feelings, desires, and conventional approaches—not on performance results data.
4. Define "needs" as gaps in resources or methods (and thus confuse ends and means).
5. Let friendly groups develop the strategic plan and thus not get internal and external performance data.
6. Target your organization itself as the primary beneficiary of the "strategic plan" and not first target external clients and society.
7. Dismiss all of this as "not practical," "not real world," or not what the "big players do."

...and you now know the reasons not to commit these errors now.

Avoiding Making Conventional Mistakes When Doing Strategic Thinking and Planning

Following is a checklist for you to use to ensure that you are staying on track.

Some Final Guidance

Possible Conventional Mistakes to Do When Doing Strategic Planning	Now Do	Will Continue to Do	Will Change What I Do
1. Call all levels of planning "strategic" and thus not aligning societal value added (Mega), organizational contributions (Macro) and value added, and individual performance contributions and value added (Micro).			
2. Use a "systems" approach (that isolates and separates the various parts of the system and treats them as if they are the entire system) and not a "system" approach, which is holistic.			
3. Confuse ends and means and blur strategy, tactics, operations, methods, and resources.			
4. Base your strategic plan only on perceptions, not also on performance-results data.			
5. Assume that there are some things that just are not measurable.			
6. Define "needs" as gaps in resources or methods (and thus confusing ends and means).			
7. Do a "training needs assessment."			
8. Let a friendly group develop the strategic plan.			

(continued)

Possible Conventional Mistakes to Do When Doing Strategic Planning	Now Do	Will Continue to Do	Will Change What I Do
9. Target your organization as the primary beneficiary of the strategic plan.			
10. Dismiss all of this as "not practical, not real world" or "because this is not what the big people do."			

Here is a checklist to further guide you in strategic planning and thinking. Make sure that you read each one:

A Mega/Strategic Planner's Checklist[6]

❑   1. Remember that one of the most painful things you can ask anyone (including yourself) to endure is change, unless you find and target the correct incentives for them to change.

❑   2. Be patient, objective, and caring. Share the possibilities and positive consequences that can and will evolve. Don't be a bully. Never accuse or abuse. Listen. Consider what people tell you. Take the approach of "come let us reason together."

❑   3. Get people away from the security of their offices and the built-in, run-and-hide excuses of being too busy to plan, answering their desk or cell phones, responding to memos, having to crank out that overdue report, or having to put out "fires." Go to a neutral area and break the ice before getting down to the realities of proactive planning. Model and build trust.

❑   4. Realize that proactive planning often carries an implied (even if unintended) criticism of the current approach, processes, regime, conventions, and culture. State that possibility very early, and get it on the table.

Some Final Guidance

☐ 5. Bring to everyone's attention that proactive strategic thinking and planning is *their* tool—their opportunity to make the kind of contribution, individually and together, they really want to deliver. Show them how they, by using proactive planning, can be in control and be the masters of change, not its victims.

☐ 6. Ask, don't tell. Don't be accusatory in your questions. Such phrases as "Isn't it possible that ..." or "I feel ..." often reduce the possibility of sending an unspoken, unwitting accusatory message.

☐ 7. Be clear. Use the language of the group, but don't change meanings only in order to have them accept you. Often people use words that are fuzzy or have too many alternative meanings. Don't water down the precision of your words and message or continually shift your meanings to fit with current biases; doing so risks falling into the "We already do that" trap. Be precise, be comfortable, maintain rigor. Get common working definitions.

☐ 8. Be patient. When people react, get defensive, start throwing off blame, or attack you, recognize and acknowledge their frustration. And realize that you might get out of your comfort zone and deal with that possibility.

☐ 9. Don't affix blame on others. Steer clear of the "we/they" divisions. Help all to envision new contributions, to set fresh horizons, and to reaffirm current useful purposes. Keep the focus on Mega: societal value added.

☐ 10. Don't take it personally when you, the "messenger," are attacked. If you have followed the above guidelines, if you are without hidden agendas, and if you really do care about the people, organization, and community you are there to help, the right results and approach will evolve. Don't forget that some people get afraid if what they are currently doing and thinking is subjected to rational alternatives.

☐ 11. Don't deviate from Mega—adding value to external clients and society—even if pressed and pushed. Mega is the practical and ethical destination.

☐ 12. Model and use the Six Critical Success Factors, the Organizational Elements Model (OEM), and the six critical success factors. Apply the six-step problem-solving process.

☐ 13. Find a sponsor, or champion, for strategic thinking and planning—the higher up in the organization and the greater their credibility, the better.

Selecting Who Should Be on the Strategic Planning Team

Who actually does the strategic planning (everyone should do strategic thinking) is vital. Here are some guidelines of whom the planning team should include:

1. Level of position power and authority; those who represent the internal and external partners
2. Level of strategic thinking and planning skills and competencies; all should think, act, and plan Mega
3. Level of commitment to the organization; don't include those who are just serving time or who have declared themselves to be "professional skeptics"
4. Level of technical expertise relevant to the core capabilities of the organization: they all should know their jobs and the jobs of others, perform magnificently, and know how all the jobs should go together to deliver success
5. Level of authentic leadership skills and competencies
6. Open, honest, and sincere behavior with no hidden objectives or single-issue agendas

Some Final Guidance

14 Basic Steps for Defining and Delivering Success: Mega Thinking and Planning[7]

Figure 10.1 illustrates the 14 steps for thinking, doing, and delivering Mega results and consequences:

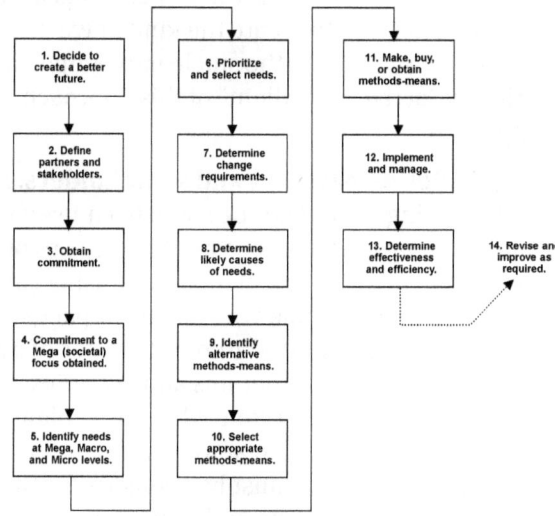

Figure 10.1. 14 Steps for defining and delivering Mega Thinking and Planning.

Let's take a look at each step briefly.

Planning

Step 1. Decide to create a better future. Mega Thinking and Planning is about improving our shared world using ourselves and our organizations as the vehicle. This proactive approach—based on helping to create the kind of world we want for tomorrow's child—is the single most important feature and is the primary "active ingredient" of this approach. It is also a unique approach.

Step 2. Define partners and stakeholders. Strategic thinking and planning should not be a lonely endeavor. If Mega Thinking and Planning is to add measurable value to our shared world, its development and implementation must be shared as well—shared with the people who will be impacted by it and the people who will implement it. Without "transfer of ownership,"[8] any plans and resulting programs and activities will be at jeopardy.

Not only does everyone who will implement and receive the consequences of Mega planning have to "buy in" to its creations and its results, there must be sponsors for the planning activities and resulting plans. The higher up in the organization you can get sponsors, the better. The sponsor(s) should be in key decision-making roles and seen by all to have credibility and the ability to support the plans once developed.[9]

Sponsors, supporters, and participants should represent those who can and will be impacted by changes or failures to change. Don't select people simply because they are friends or are politically connected. Everyone should know that Mega Thinking and Planning is bias-free.

Steps 3 and 4. Get commitment. No lip-service or passive support: get all the players to actually commit and sign off. The strategic thinking and planning agreement in Table 10.1. can get you started to make sure that all involved partners agree on Mega and the linkages among levels of results and consequences.

Some Final Guidance

Step 5. Identify needs at the Mega, Macro, and Micro levels. Because organizations must link external client and societal contributions (Mega) with organizational contributions (Macro) and individual and small group contributions (Micro), needs—gaps in results—at each level must be harvested.

Needs at the Mega level should be based on the Ideal Vision (Figure 3.1), and these gaps in results will serve to provide you with the Mission Objective. The Mission Objective is the measurable statement of what your organization will deliver to move it ever-closer to the needs identified in the Ideal Vision. Figure 7.1 shows how the various levels are linked and related as you move from Mega to Macro to Micro.

Step 6. Prioritize and select needs. Because needs are gaps in results, prioritization should be done on the basis of costs-consequences assessment; the cost to meet the needs as compared to the costs for ignoring them. Needs should be prioritized at the Mega, Macro, and Micro levels. Guides for prioritizing selected needs are provided in Chapter 5.

Step 7. Determine change requirements. This step asks that you compare your current results and methods-means with the required ones so that you may identify what should be changed in your organization (results, resources, methods, etc.) and what you should keep and maintain. The priorities derived in step 6 above provide the criteria.

Step 8. Determine likely causes of the needs. Now that you have identified the changes and what should be continued, you can do an analysis of what is causing the gaps in results for the needs you want to reduce or eliminate. For example, current levees in New Orleans might contain the ravages of a category 3 storm and you want them to resist a category 4 storm. What are the causes of current failures? Politics, fraud, engineering, funding, commitment, cooperation, maintenance? This is where you find the reasons for the current priority gaps so that you can identify what must change.

Step 9. Identify alternative methods and means. Now you survey all of the possible ways and means to close the gaps in results—needs—you have selected and list the advantages and disadvantages of each. For example one methods-means would be government funding of levee reconstruction. An advantage would be in the immediacy of funds. A possible disadvantage could be that any funding would be wasted.

Doing

Step 10. Select the appropriate methods and means. This is getting into the implementation of the strategic/Mega plan. Based on costs-consequences (what you get and what you give) you pick the most effective and efficient ways and resources to meet the needs.

Step 11. Make or buy or obtain the methods and means. This is more of implementation; as the athletic footwear ads note "Just do it." There are many performance design, development, and implementation approaches available for this.

Step 12. Implement and manage. Against the performance criteria developed earlier, ensure that everything stays on course, stays on schedule, and meets all requirements. If not developing appropriately, revise as required.

Step 13. Determine effectiveness and efficiency. This is a summative evaluation. You compare your results with your objectives and identify what worked and what did not, all based on measurable criteria and performance.

Step 14. Revise as required. Each short-fall is a friend in disguise, for it tells you what must be changed to deliver success. Evaluation (Step 13 above) should never be for blaming but fixing, and here is where the fixing can happen. Change what should be changed and keep what is working. This step is actually done both at this stage of planning and doing as well as at each of the previous steps.

Some Final Guidance

Definitions of all terms are in the Glossary section at the end of this book.

Agreement is not a solitary enterprise. In a system, where all the parts interact and together move to a common and shared destination, it is vital that everyone agrees on Mega Thinking and Planning. In order to get everyone to commit to Mega Thinking and Planning, use the following agreement table in Table 10.1.

Mega/Strategic Thinking and Planning Agreement Table	COMMITMENT			
	Clients		Planners	
	Y	N	Y	N
1. The total organization will contribute to clients' and societal survival, health, and well-being.				
2. The total organization will contribute to clients' societal quality of life.				
3. Clients' and societal survival, health, and well-being will be part of the organization's and each of its facility's mission objectives.				
4. Each organizational operation function will have objectives that contribute to #1, #2, and #3.				
5. Each job/task will have objectives that contribute to #1, #2, #3, and #4.				
6. A needs assessment will identify and document any gaps in results at the operational levels of #1, #2, #3, #4, and #5.				
7. Human resources/training and/or operations requirements will be based on the needs identified and selected in #6.				
8. The results of #6 may recommend non-HRD/training interventions.				
9. Evaluation and continual improvement will compare results with objectives for #1, #2, #3, #4, and #5.				

Table 10.1. An agreement table for Mega Thinking and Planning that can be used to gain consensus.[10]

Ask each person, including all internal and external stakeholders to actually "sign off" on each of their choices. Require that each person chooses "yes" or "no." If someone has questions such as definitions or other problems, just tell them to sign "no" to that item. As you move through these questions, soon it will be apparent to all (except for the most intractable people who don't get hung up on facts and reality), that Mega Thinking and Planning is essential for success.[11]

Assessing Your Progress

Mega Thinking and Planning can make you and your organization successful. The choice to do it is up to you. The Pocket Guide has given you the basics. This is a good time to compare where you started in Chapter 1 with where you are now in terms of using Mega Thinking and Planning to create a new future for defining and delivering success.

WHAT IS					STRATEGIC THINKING AND PLANNING SURVEY	WHAT SHOULD BE				
1 - Rarely, if ever	2 - Not usually	3 - Sometimes	4 - Frequently	5 - Consistently	Respond to each item below using the following scale. Use this scale for both **What Is** and **What Should Be**. 1 – Rarely, if ever 2 – Not usually 3 – Sometimes 4 – Frequently 5 – Consistently	1 - Rarely, if ever	2 - Not usually	3 - Sometimes	4 - Frequently	5 - Consistently
①	②	③	④	⑤	1. Planning has a focus on creating the future.	①	②	③	④	⑤
①	②	③	④	⑤	2. We define *strategic planning* as starting with an initial focus on measurable societal value added.	①	②	③	④	⑤
①	②	③	④	⑤	3. We define *tactical planning* as having a focus on measurable organizational value added.	①	②	③	④	⑤
①	②	③	④	⑤	4. We define *operational planning* as having a focus on measurable individual and small group value added.	①	②	③	④	⑤

(continued)

Some Final Guidance

Respond to each item below using the following scale. Use this scale for both **What Is** and **What Should Be**.

1 – Rarely, if ever
2 – Not usually
3 – Sometimes
4 – Frequently
5 – Consistently

WHAT IS	STRATEGIC THINKING AND PLANNING SURVEY	WHAT SHOULD BE
① ② ③ ④ ⑤	5. We start *strategic planning and thinking* at the societal value-added level.	① ② ③ ④ ⑤
① ② ③ ④ ⑤	6. In our strategic planning, we carefully distinguish among strategic, tactical, and operational planning.	① ② ③ ④ ⑤
① ② ③ ④ ⑤	7. We align—link and relate—strategic, tactical, and operational planning.	① ② ③ ④ ⑤
① ② ③ ④ ⑤	8. All people in our organization understand the differences and relationships among strategic, tactical, and operational planning.	① ② ③ ④ ⑤
① ② ③ ④ ⑤	9. Planning involves, either directly or indirectly, all those people and parties who will be impacted by the results of the strategic plan.	① ② ③ ④ ⑤
① ② ③ ④ ⑤	10. Planning always focuses on results.	① ② ③ ④ ⑤
① ② ③ ④ ⑤	11. Planning has always focused on the consequences of achieving (or not achieving) results.	① ② ③ ④ ⑤
① ② ③ ④ ⑤	12. Planning is proactive.	① ② ③ ④ ⑤
① ② ③ ④ ⑤	13. Revisions to the plan are made any time it is required.	① ② ③ ④ ⑤
① ② ③ ④ ⑤	14. We use an Ideal Vision—the kind of world we want to help create for tomorrow's child—as the basis for planning.	① ② ③ ④ ⑤
① ② ③ ④ ⑤	15. People who are involved and could be impacted by the plans participate in the planning.	① ② ③ ④ ⑤

(continued)

The Manager's Pocket Guide to Mega Thinking and Planning

Respond to each item below using the following scale. Use this scale for both **What Is** and **What Should Be**.

1 – Rarely, if ever
2 – Not usually
3 – Sometimes
4 – Frequently
5 – Consistently

WHAT IS	STRATEGIC THINKING AND PLANNING SURVEY	WHAT SHOULD BE
① ② ③ ④ ⑤	16. We use a formal needs assessment—collecting and prioritizing gaps in results—for making plans.	① ② ③ ④ ⑤
① ② ③ ④ ⑤	17. We collect needs at all three levels of planning: strategic, tactical, and operational.	① ② ③ ④ ⑤
	18. When we do strategic planning, we formally consider and collect data for the following Ideal Vision purposes:	
① ② ③ ④ ⑤	a) There will be no losses of life or elimination or reduction of levels of well-being, survival, self-sufficiency, or quality of life from any source.	① ② ③ ④ ⑤
① ② ③ ④ ⑤	b) Eliminate terrorism, illegal civil protest, war, and/or riot.	① ② ③ ④ ⑤
① ② ③ ④ ⑤	c) Eliminate unintended human-caused changes to the environment including permanent destruction of the environment and/or rendering it nonrenewable.	① ② ③ ④ ⑤
① ② ③ ④ ⑤	d) Eliminate murder, rape, or crimes of violence, robbery, or destruction of property.	① ② ③ ④ ⑤
① ② ③ ④ ⑤	e) Eliminate disabling substance abuse.	① ② ③ ④ ⑤
① ② ③ ④ ⑤	f) Eliminate disabling diseases.	① ② ③ ④ ⑤
① ② ③ ④ ⑤	g) Eliminate starvation and/or malnutrition.	① ② ③ ④ ⑤

(continued)

Some Final Guidance

Respond to each item below using the following scale. Use this scale for both **What Is** and **What Should Be**.

1 – Rarely, if ever
2 – Not usually
3 – Sometimes
4 – Frequently
5 – Consistently

WHAT IS	STRATEGIC THINKING AND PLANNING SURVEY	WHAT SHOULD BE
① ② ③ ④ ⑤	19. The elements of the Ideal Vision (a through g above) are treated as interrelated, not just each one independently.	① ② ③ ④ ⑤
① ② ③ ④ ⑤	20. Planning is done before taking action.	① ② ③ ④ ⑤
① ② ③ ④ ⑤	21. Plans are used when making decisions.	① ② ③ ④ ⑤

Table 1.1. (repeated from Chapter 1).
Defining What Is and What Should Be for
gaining commitment to Mega Thinking and Planning.

Compare your response in Chapter 1 with where you and your organization are now. See, change is possible and useful!

* * * * *

Apply all that is in this Manager's Pocket Guide and create success that you can prove. It will allow you to be successful in the realities of change, choices, and consequences.

It works.

Endnotes

1. Based in part on Kaufman, R., & Clark, R. (Oct., 1999). Re-establishing performance improvement as a legitimate area of inquiry, activity, and contribution: Rules of the road. *Performance Improvement, 38*(9), pp. 13–18.

2. President Harry S. Truman used this as his guide to make decisions and take actions.

3. Mega, Macro, and Micro are not code for big, smaller, and smallest.

4. Recall that these three types of results are blurred in our literature. It would seem that every result is called an "outcome" and thus obscures the importance of three related types of results as well as the consequences and value added of each.

5. Based on Kaufman, R. (2006). Seven stupid things people do when they attempt strategic thinking and planning. In Silberman, R., & Phillips, P. *The 2006 ASTD Organization Development and Leadership Sourcebook.* Alexandria, VA.

6. Based in part on Kaufman, R., Oakley-Browne, H., Watkins, R. & Leigh, D. (2003). *Practical strategic planning: Aligning people, performance, and payoffs.* San Francisco, CA: Jossey-Bass/Pfeiffer.

7. This 14-step process for achieving high impact—Mega results—was inspired by Kaufman and Stone (1982), and also provided in Kaufman, R., Oakley-Brown, H., Watkins, R., & Leigh, D. (2003).

Some Final Guidance

8. This concept is from Drucker, P. F. (1973). *Management: tasks, responsibilities, practices.* New York: Harper & Row.
9. Some basics on this may be found in Lick, D., & Kaufman, R. (Winter, 2000–2001). Change creation: The rest of the planning story. *Planning for Higher Education, 29*(2), pp. 24–36; Roberts, W. (1987). *Leadership Secrets of Attila the Hun.* New York: Warner; Conner, D. R. (1992). *Managing at the speed of change.* New York: Villard Books, Division of Random House; Conner, D. R. (1998). *Building nimble organizations.* New York: John Wiley & Sons, among other sources on change and leadership.
10. Based on Kaufman, R. (2000). *Mega Planning: Practical tools for organizational success.* Thousand Oaks, CA: Sage Publications. Also *Planificación Mega: Herramientas practices paral el exito organizacional.* (2004). Traducción de Sonia Agut. Universitat Jaume I. Castelló de la Plana, Espana.
11. Based on Kaufman, R., & Guerra-Lopez, I. (2008). *The assessment book: Applied strategic thinking and performance improvement through self-assessments.* Amherst, MA: HRD Press, Inc.

Glossary of Terms

System, Systems, Systematic, and Systemic: related but not the same.

system approach: Begins with the sum total of parts working independently and together to achieve a useful set of results at the societal level...adding value for all internal and external partners. We best think of it as the large whole and we can show it thus:

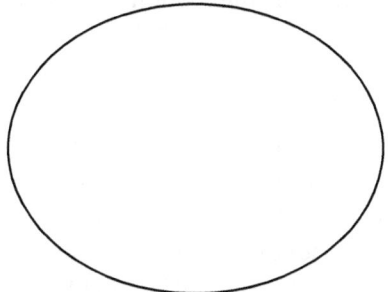

systems approach: Begins with the parts of a system—subsystems—that make up the "system." We can show it thus:

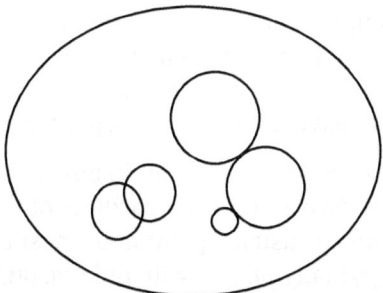

The "system" is made up of smaller elements, or subsystems, shown as "bubbles" embedded in the larger system. If we start at this smaller level, we will start with a part and not the whole. So when someone says they are using a "systems approach," they are really focusing on one or more subsystems—they are unfortunately focusing on the parts and not the whole. When planning and doing at this level, they can only assume that the payoffs and consequences will add up to something useful to society and external clients, and this is usually a very big assumption.

systematic approach: An approach that does things in an orderly, predictable, and controlled manner. It is a reproducible process. Doing things, however, in a systematic manner does not ensure the achievement of useful results.

systemic approach: An approach that affects everything in the system. The definition of "the system" is usually left up to the practitioner and may or may not include external clients and society. It does not necessarily mean that when something is systemic it is also useful.

change creation: The definition and justification, proactively, of new and justified as well as justifiable destinations. If this is done before change management, acceptance is more likely. This is a proactive orientation for change and differs from the more usual "change management" in that it identifies in advance where individuals and organizations are headed rather than waiting for change to occur and be "managed."

change management: Ensuring that whatever change is selected will be accepted and implemented successfully by people in the organization. Change management is reactive in that it waits until change requirements are either defined or imposed and then moves to have the change accepted and used.

comfort zones: The psychological areas, in business or in life, where one feels secure and safe (regardless of the reality of that feeling). Change is usually painful for most people. When faced with change, many people will find reasons (usually not rational) for why not to make any modifications.

costs-consequences analysis: The process of estimating a return-on-investment analysis before an intervention is implemented. It asks two basic questions simultaneously: what do you expect to give and what do you expect to get back in terms of results? Most formulations do not compute costs and

Glossary of Terms

consequences for society and external client (Mega) return-on-investment. Thus, even the calculations for standard approaches steer away from the vital consideration of self-sufficiency, health, and well-being.

criteria: Precise and rigorous specifications that allow one to prove what has been or has to be accomplished. Many processes in place today do not use rigorous indicators for expected performance. If criteria are "loose" or unclear, there is no realistic basis for evaluation and continuous improvement. Loose criteria often meets the comfort-test but doesn't allow for the humanistic approach to care enough about others to define, with stakeholders, where you are headed and how to tell when you have or have not arrived.

deep change: Change that extends from Mega—societal value added—downward into the organization to define and shape Macro, Micro, Processes, and Inputs. It is termed "deep change" to note that it is not superficial or just cosmetic, or even a splintered quick fix. Most planning models do not include Mega results in the change process and thus miss the opportunity to find out what impact their contributions and results have on external clients and society. The other approaches might be termed "superficial change" or "limited change" in that they only focus on an organization or a small part of an organization.

desired results: Ends (or results) identified through needs assessments that are derived from soft data relating to "perceived needs." "Desired" indicates these are perceptual and personal in nature.

ends: Results, achievements, consequences, payoffs, and/or impacts. The more precise the results, the more likely that reasonable methods and means can be considered, implemented, and evaluated. Without rigor for results statements, confusion can take the place of successful performance.

evaluation: Compares current status (what is) with intended status (what was intended) and is most commonly done only after an intervention is implemented. Unfortunately, "evaluation" is frequently used for blaming and not fixing or improving. When blame follows evaluation, people tend to avoid the means and criteria for evaluation or leave them so loose that any result can be explained away.

evidence-based management: An evolving approach in the last two decades that encourages using the best available scientific evidence and actual performance data and results in making decisions.

external needs assessment: Determining and prioritizing gaps in results, then selecting problems to be resolved at the Mega level. This level of needs assessment is most often missing from conventional approaches. Without the data from it, one cannot be assured that there will be strategic alignment from internal results to external value added.

hard data: Performance data that is based on objectives and is independently verifiable. This type of data is critical. It should be used along with "soft" or perception data.

Ideal Vision: The measurable definition of the kind of world we, together with others, commit to help deliver for tomorrow's child. An Ideal Vision defines the Mega level of planning. It allows an organization and all of its partners to define where they are headed and how to tell when they are getting there or getting closer. It provides the rationality and reasons for an organizational mission objective.

Inputs: The ingredients, raw materials, and physical and human resources that an organization can use in its processes in order to deliver useful ends. These ingredients and resources are often the only considerations made during planning... without determining the value they add internally and external to the organization.

Glossary of Terms

internal needs assessment: Determining and prioritizing gaps, then selecting problems to be resolved at the Micro and Macro levels. Most needs assessment processes are of this variety.

Macro level of planning: Planning focused on the organization itself as the primary client and beneficiary of what is planned and delivered. This is the conventional starting and stopping place for existing planning approaches.

means: Processes, activities, resources, methods, or techniques used to deliver a result. Means are only useful to the extent that they deliver useful results at all three levels of planned results: Mega, Macro, and Micro.

Mega level of planning (system approach): Planning focused on external clients, including customers/citizens and the community and society that the organization serves. This is the usual missing planning level in most formulations. It is the only one that will focus on societal value added: survival, self-sufficiency, and quality of life of all partners. It is suggested that this type of planning is imperative for getting and proving useful results.

Mega thinking: A mindset or way of viewing the world—thinking about every situation, problem, or opportunity in terms of what you use, do, produce, and deliver as having to add value to external clients and society. Same as strategic thinking.

methods-means analysis: Identifies possible tactics and tools for meeting the needs identified in a "system analysis." The methods-means analysis identifies the possible ways and means to meet the needs and achieve the detailed objectives that are identified in this Mega plan, but does not select them. Interestingly, this is a comfortable place where some operational planning starts. Thus, it either assumes or ignores the requirement to measurably add value within and outside the organization.

Micro-level planning: Planning focused on individuals or small groups (such as desired and required competencies of associates or supplier competencies). Planning for building-block results. This also is a comfortable place where some operational planning starts. Starting here usually assumes or ignores the requirement to measurably add value to the entire organization as well as to outside the organization.

mission objective: An exact, performance-based statement of an organization's overall intended results that it can and should deliver to external clients and society. A mission objective is measurable on an Interval or Ratio scale, so it states not only "where are we headed" but also adds "how we will know when we have arrived." A mission objective is best linked to Mega levels of planning and the Ideal Vision to ensure societal value added.

mission statement: An organization's Macro-level "general purpose," a mission statement is only measurable on a Nominal or Ordinal scale of measurement and only states "where are we headed" and provides no rigorous criteria for determining how one measures successful accomplishment.

need: The gap between current results and desired or required results. This is where a lot of planning "goes off the rails." By defining any gap as a "need," one fails to distinguish between means and ends and thus confuses what and how. If "need" is defined as a gap in results, then there is a triple bonus: (1) it states the objectives (What Should Be), (2) it contains the evaluation and continuous improvement criteria (What Should Be), and (3) it provides the basis for justifying any proposal by using both ends of a need—What Is and What Should Be in terms of results. Proof can be given for the costs to meet the need as well as the costs to ignore the need.

needs analysis: Taking the determined gaps between adjacent Organizational Elements, and finding the causes of the inability for delivering required results. A needs analysis also identifies possible ways and means to close the gaps in results—needs—but does not select them. Unfortunately, "needs

Glossary of Terms

analysis" is usually used interchangeable with "needs assessment." They are not the same. How does one "analyze" something (such as a need) before they know what should be analyzed? First assess the needs, and then analyze it.

needs assessment: A formal process that identifies and documents gaps between current and desired and/or required results, arranges them in order of priority on basis of the cost to meet the need as compared to the cost of ignoring it, and selects problems to be resolved. By starting with a needs assessment, justifiable performance data and the gaps between What Is and What Should Be will provide the realistic and rational reason for both what to change as well as what to continue.

objectives: Precise statement of purpose or destination of where are we headed and how will we be able to tell when we have arrived; the four parts to an objective are (1) what result is to be demonstrated, (2) who or what will demonstrate the result, (3) where will the result be observed, (4) what Interval or Ratio scale criteria will be used. Loose or process-oriented objectives will confuse everyone. All results, including those at the Mega, Macro, and Micro levels are stated as an objective.

Outcomes: Results and payoffs at the external client and societal level. Outcomes are results that add value to society, community, and external clients of the organization. These are results at the Mega level of planning.

Outputs: The results and payoffs that an organization can or does deliver outside of itself to external clients and society. These are results at the Macro level of planning where the primary client and beneficiary is the organization itself. It does not formally link to Outcomes and societal well-being unless it is derived from Outcomes and the Ideal (Mega) Vision.

paradigm: The framework and ground rules individuals use to filter reality and understand the world around them. It is vital that people have common paradigms that guide them. That is one of the functions of the Mega level of planning and Outcomes so that everyone is headed to a common destination and may uniquely contribute to that journey.

performance: A result or consequence of any intervention or activity, including individual, team, or organization. An end.

performance accomplishment system (PAS): Any of a variety of interventions (such as "instructional systems design and development," quality management/continuous improvement, benchmarking, reengineering, and the like) that are results oriented and are intended to get positive results. These are usually focused at the Micro/Products level. This is my preferred alternative to the rather sterile term "performance technology" that often steers people toward hardware and premature solutions.

Processes: The means, processes, activities, procedures, interventions, programs, and initiatives an organization can or does use in order to deliver useful ends. While most planners start here, it is dangerous not to derive the Processes and Inputs from what an organization must deliver and the payoffs for external clients.

Products: The building-block results and payoffs of individuals and small groups that form the basis of what an organization produces and delivers inside as well as outside of itself, and the payoffs for external clients and society. Products are results at the Micro level of planning.

quasi-need: A gap in a method, resource, or process. Many so-called "needs assessments" are really quasi needs assessments since they tend to pay immediate attention to means (such as training) before defining and justifying the ends and consequences.

Glossary of Terms

required results: Ends identified through needs assessment that are derived from hard data relating to objective performance measures.

Results: Ends, Products, Outputs, Outcomes; accomplishments and consequences. Usually misses the Outputs and Outcomes.

soft data: Personal perceptions of results. Soft data is not independently verifiable. While people's perceptions are reality for them, they are not to be relied on without relating to hard—independently verifiable—data as well.

strategic alignment: The linking of Mega, Macro, and Micro level planning and results with each other and with Processes and Inputs. By formally deriving what the organization uses, does, produces, and delivers to Mega/external payoffs, strategic alignment is complete.

strategic thinking: Approaching any problem, program, project, activity, or effort with noting that everything that is used, done, produced, and delivered must add value for external clients and society. Strategic thinking starts with Mega.

tactical planning: Finding out what is available to get from What Is to What Should Be at the organizational/Macro level. Tactics are best identified after the overall mission has been selected based on its linkages and contributions to external client and societal (Ideal Vision) results and consequences.

wants: Preferred methods and means assumed to be capable of meeting needs.

What Is: Current operational results and consequences; these could be for an individual, an organization, and/or a society.

What Should Be: Desired or required operational results and consequences; these could be for an individual, an organization and/or a society.

wishes: Desires concerning means and ends. It is important not to confuse "wishes" with needs.

About the Author

Roger Kaufman is professor emeritus, educational psychology and learning systems, and was director, Office for Needs Assessment and Planning, as well as Associate Director of the Learning Systems Institute, all at the Florida State University (1975–2003) where he received the Professorial Excellence Award. He is also Distinguished Research Professor at the Sonora Institute of Technology (Mexico) and consulting faculty in business and technology at Excelsior College. Kaufman has served as Research Professor of Engineering Management at the Old Dominion University as well as the New Jersey Institute of Technology and associated with the faculty of industrial engineering at the University of Central Florida. In addition, he is Director of Roger Kaufman & Associates. Kaufman is a Certified Performance Technologist, International Society for Performance Improvement. He received the U.S. Coast Guard/Department of Homeland Security medal for Meritorious Public Service. Previously he was professor of human behavior at the United States International University (now Alliant International University) and professor of education at Chapman University, and also taught courses in strategic planning, needs assessment, and evaluation at the University of Southern California and Pepperdine University. He was the 1983 Haydn Williams Fellow at the Curtin University of Technology in Perth, Australia. Roger serves as the Vice Chair of the Senior Research Advisory Committee for Florida TaxWatch. His Ph.D. in communications is from New York University, with additional graduate work in industrial engineering, psychology, and education at the University of California at Berkeley and Johns Hopkins University (MA). His undergraduate work was in psychology, statistics, sociology, and industrial engineering at Purdue and George Washington (BA) Universities.

Before entering higher education, he was Assistant to the Vice President for Engineering as well as Assistant to the Vice President for Research at Douglas Aircraft Company. Prior to that, he was Director of Training System Analysis at U.S. Industries; Head of Training Systems for the New York office of Bolt, Beranek & Newman; and head of human factors engineering at Martin Baltimore and earlier as a human factors specialist at Boeing. He has served two terms on the U.S. Secretary of the Navy's Advisory Board on Education and Training.

Kaufman's clients—working in the areas of strategic planning, change management–change creation, quality management, needs assessment, evaluation, distance learning, and organizational improvement include or have included:

Accenture
Accounting Firms Associated
American Airlines Group/Blue Cross of Texas/ISPI
American Association of School Administrators (AASA)—National Academy of School Executives (NASE)
Arthur Andersen and Andersen Consulting (World headquarters and Australia)
AT&T
Australian Department of Defence
Australian Public Service and Merit Protection Commission
Australian Treasury
Bank of Boston (Argentina)
Bankers' Institute of New Zealand
Bell Canada
Boatmen's Bancshares
Boeing Leadership Center
Boeing/Microsoft/ISPI
Boise State University
Box Hill Institute of TAFE (Australia)
Catholic University of Chile
Catholic University of Valparaiso (Chile)
Central Statistical Office (UK)
Chase Manhattan Bank
Council of Chief State School Officers
Deutsche Bank
EastConn Regional Education Service Center
Edison Community College
Equifax
Excelsior College
Fireman's Fund Insurance
First Union Bank
Flight Safety International
Florida Department of Corrections
Florida Department of Education
Florida Department of Environmental Protection
Florida Department of Health & Rehabilitative Services
Florida Governor's Office of Planning and Budget
Florida Office of Tobacco Control
Florida Power & Light
Gallaudet University
Hugh Oakley-Browne Associates
IBM
Institute of Educational Technology/Ministry of Culture and Education of Argentina
International Society for Performance Improvement

About the Author

Leon County (Florida) School Board
Los Alamos National Laboratories
M&M Mars
March of Dimes
MBC (Argentina & Chicago)
McDonnell-Douglas
McGraw-Hill
Microsoft
Milliken Industries
MIM Holdings, Ltd.
Moran Towing
National Open University of Venezuela
New Zealand Department of Health
New Zealand departments of Minister and Cabinet, Treasury, Army, State Services, and Science and Technology
New Zealand Universities Academic Audit Unit
Niagara Wires Division of Niagara-Lockport
Nova Southeastern University
Ohio Civil Service Employees Association/AFL-CIO
Otago Polytechnic (New Zealand)
Parke-Davis
Pasa Petrochemical and Refinor (Argentina)
Perez Companc S. A.
Pew Charitable Trusts
Pioneer Cement
Polytechnic University of Ecuador (ESPOL)
Prairie-View A&M University
Prevention First
Shell Oil Company
Simon Bolivar University
Sonora Institute of Technology (Mexico)
State University of New York
Sun Microsystems
Sydney Water Board
Texas Instruments
Train-Koeln (Germany)
Tricon Global Industries (Pizza Hut, Taco Bell, KFC)
U.S. Army Training & Doctrine Command/Comtech
U.S. Army Training Support Center
U.S. Centers for Disease Control
U.S. Coast Guard
U.S. Department of Education
U.S. Department of Veterans Affairs
U.S. Department of Veterans Affairs/Veterans Benefits Administration
U.S. Marine Corps
Unisys of Australia
Universidades Tecnologicas (Mexico)
University of Puerto Rico
Valencia (Florida) Community College
Venezuela American Society for Curriculum and Development (ASCD)
Vice Chancellor and Chief of Staff
Wellington (New Zealand) City Council
World Bank

He was a member of the Board of Directors of the Florida Governor's Humanities Council and is a member of the advisory board of the Center for Measuring University Performance at the Arizona State University.

Kaufman is a Fellow of the American Psychological Association, a Fellow of the American Academy of School Psychology, a Fellow of the American Educational Research Association, and a Diplomat of the American Board of Professional Psychology. He has been awarded the highest honor of the International Society for Performance Improvement by being named an honorary "Member for Life," an organization for which he also served as president. He has been awarded the Thomas F. Gilbert Professional Achievement Award by that same organization. He is also the recipient of the Distinguished Contribution to Workplace Learning and Performance, American Society for Training and Development (ASTD), and Asia Pacific Human Resources Management 2007–2008 Leadership Award.

Kaufman has published 40 books, including:

- *30 Seconds that Can Change Your Life: A Decision-Making Guide for Those who Refuse to Be Mediocre*
- *Change, Choice, and Consequences: A Guide to Strategic Thinking and Planning*
- *The Assessment Book: Applied Strategic Thinking and Performance Improvement through Self-Assessments*
- *Mega Planning*
- *Strategic Thinking—Revised*

He co-authored *Useful Educational Results: Defining, Prioritizing, and Accomplishing*, as well as *Practical Strategic Planning: Aligning People, Performance, and Payoffs* and *Practical Evaluation for Educators: Finding What Works and What Doesn't*. He has also published 275 articles on strategic planning, performance improvement, distance learning, quality management and continual improvement, needs assessment, management, and evaluation.

Contacts: 1123 Lasswade Drive, Tallahassee, FL 32312, USA
Phone: (850) 386-6321   **Fax:** (850) 422-2722
E-mail: rkaufman@nettally.com   **Website:** megaplanning.com

www.ingramcontent.com/pod-product-compliance
Lightning Source LLC
Chambersburg PA
CBHW071704090426
42738CB00009B/1655